I0569645

Figure 1: Guru Nanak with Japuji Sahib inscribed
all over. Creator unknown, 1880/1900.

ਜਪੁਜੀ ਸਾਹਿਬ

JAPUJI

Hymn of Guru Nanak

translated by

Om Prakash Bakshi

edited by

Vivek Bakshi

RUHANI
PUBLICATIONS

AUSTIN, TX

ਜਪੁਜੀ ਸਾਹਿਬ

JAPUJI

Hymn of Guru Nanak

Translation Copyright © 2025 by Vivek Bakshi
Edited by Vivek Bakshi
All rights reserved.

Japuji Sahib is a sacred text composed by Guru Nanak (1469–1539) and is in the public domain. The translation and commentary presented here reflect the translator's personal understanding and interpretation of the original Gurmukhi text. They are not intended as an official or doctrinal version. Readers are encouraged to consult multiple sources for a fuller understanding of the scripture.

Fonts from Adobe
Cover images from Shutterstock
In all cases, photo attribution has been noted. Please direct any inquiries on photo usage to drvivekbakshi@ruhanipublications.com.

All rights reserved. This book may not be reproduced in any manner whatsoever without express permission of the copyright holder.

A Ruhani Publications Book
Austin, TX, USA
For more information, write:
info@ruhanipublications.com
www.ruhanipublications.com

ISBN: 978-1-970413-00-7 (paperback)
ISBN: 978-1-970413-01-4 (hardcover)

Dedicated to the loving memory of my late father to whom I attribute the development of my present taste of yearning to know more and more about spiritual wealth.

And to my wife, Pushpa Bakshi, MA (Punjabi) and *Gyani*, with whom I had many fruitful discussions regarding this translation.

table of contents

Figure 2: Fresco of Guru Nanak from Baoli Sahib, Goindwal
Creator unknown, circa 19th century.

acknowledgement

In my endeavor to understand the original text of *Japuji*, I read most of the available commentaries and translations in English, Urdu and Panjabi. I am, therefore, indebted to the writers of all of them in general. I am, however, particularly indebted to Sant Kirpal Singh from whose translation of *Japuji* I have quoted in a place or two.

Figure 3: Coin from 1747 CE depicting Guru Nanak with his two disciples.

the preface

GURU NANAK, THE FIRST OF THE TEN SIKH GURUS, WAS born in the year of 1469 A.D. Born in a Hindu family of the Panjab, he never professed to belong to any particular religion. He was an embodiment of universal brotherhood. He stood for the whole of humanity. His soul yearned to serve Man rather than men, and he toured extensively on foot, spreading his divine message to ailing humanity, irrespective of caste and creed.

Japuji, the beautiful hymn of Guru Nanak, forms the first chapter of Guru Granth Sahib—the holy scripture of the Sikhs. It contains the fundamental principles of Guru Nanak's teachings. In the very outset it deals with the basic question: How to attain realization?

The verse of Japuji is composed most exquisitely in the Panjabi of the 15th century. Ordinarily, it eludes any attempt at translating it. Obviously, any effort to translate such a text in poetry even by a consummate artist, though it will be of a definite literary value, cannot capture the original luster. Again, a literal translation, though desirable with a view to preserving the originality of the text, cannot hope to convey clearly to the reader the correct interpretation of such a text as Japuji. I have, therefore, taken to rendering free translation in English prose of this rare text.

Om Prakash Bakshi

3

editor's introduction

IT IS MY PLEASURE TO SHARE THE ROOTS OF THIS PROJECT: my ancestral/familial background that resulted in this present translation, followed by needed notes on the publication of the current version.

Japuji Sahib has deep roots within my family. If I ever woke up before dawn, I could hear my mother, Pushpa Bakshi, reciting it in a low voice with her head covered in a dupatta and with *shri gutka sahib* (small hymn book with a blue cover) in her hand, even though she had already committed the passages to memory, as did her mother, my Nani ji, Kartar Singh, a Sikh who devoted large parts of her day reciting it. In fact, whenever, I saw her, she had *shri gutka sahib* in her hand, which comforted me as a boy, and now as grown man, thinking about the legacy of what my son, Taru Om Arun Bakshi, will inherit from my lineage, from elders who passed long before he was born, here in America—in Austin, Texas.

Japuji Sahib also has deep connections within my father's side of the family, but in a different way than my mother's. My father, Om Prakash Bakshi's approach to life was more intellectual; he always wanted to look deeply into the meaning and significance of things. Recently, I discovered a copy of the Bhagavad Gita with his signatures and markings from 1952, where he was looking for meaning of original words in Sanskrit. I traced my fingers on his handwriting and it felt like he was in

4

the room with me, accompanying me on the late nights I spent in my office, poring over Sanskrit Texts that enlightened me and took me deeper into contemplative thought.

My mother possessed the degree of Gyani, which authorized her to recite the holy scripture Guru Granth Sahib, which she occasionally did while teaching in Guru Nanak Girls College in Lucknow. In the 1970s, when she pursued her master's in Punjabi, my father joined her in her studies. I remember them discussing various topics in detail—one such topic was the meaning of words of Japuji Sahib. Many of their discussions revolved around this translation.

The publication of this translation is long overdue. I have made minimal additions to it, merely for the sake of publishing it in a book format. On the suggestion of my editor, Dan McGowan, I have added a glossary. I also wish to thank my friend Anmol P Paralkar who had fixed typos in English and Gurmukhi texts. In the original manuscript, the Gurmukhi text was handwritten, and I have typeset it for the entire manuscript. I would like to thank P. J. Hoover for the design and layout expertise, for her keen eye and ongoing energy for this project. Finally, I'd like to thank my wife, Bethany Hegedus Bakshi, and daughter Emily Heider, who always applaud my accomplishments and have long supported the vision of bringing this book to life.

May what follows offer you a deeper respect and knowledge of Japuji Sahib, which carries essence of Guru Granth Sahib, like Upanishads do for Vedas.

Vivek Bakshi (Editor)
November 11, 2025, Austin, Texas, USA

Figure 4: From a 17th-century copy of the Guru Granth Sahib.

ਜਪੁਜੀ ਸਾਹਿਬ

JAPUJI

Hymn of Guru Nanak

ੴ ਸਤਿਨਾਮੁ ਕਰਤਾ ਪੁਰਖੁ ਨਿਰਭਉ ਨਿਰਵੈਰੁ
ਅਕਾਲ ਮੂਰਤਿ ਅਜੂਨੀ ਸੈਭੰ ਗੁਰਪ੍ਰਸਾਦਿ॥

॥ਜਪੁ॥

ਆਦਿ ਸਚੁ ਜੁਗਾਦਿ ਸਚੁ ॥
ਹੈ ਭੀ ਸਚੁ ਨਾਨਕ ਹੋਸੀ ਭੀ ਸਚੁ॥੧॥

the prologue

THE OPENING VERSE IS A SORT OF INVOCATION TO GOD THE Almighty and recurs subsequently also in the other compositions in the *Holy Granth*. It runs:

> There is only one God the Almighty. He is the only immortal being. He is beyond fear, beyond enmity, beyond time, and beyond birth and death. Contact to Him can be had through the grace of Guru.

Guru Nanak further elucidates God the Almighty invoked by him in the preceding verse in the following words:

> He was present before all ages began. He existed throughout all ages. He exists even now, and shall continue to exist ever hereafter.

ਸੋਚੈ ਸੋਚਿ ਨ ਹੋਵਈ ਜੇ ਸੋਚੀ ਲਖ ਵਾਰ॥

ਚੁਪੈ ਚੁਪਿ ਨ ਹੋਵਈ ਜੇ ਲਾਇ ਰਹਾ ਲਿਵ ਤਾਰ॥

ਭੁਖਿਆ ਭੁਖ ਨ ਉਤਰੀ ਜੇ ਬੰਨਾ ਪੁਰੀਆ ਭਾਰ॥

ਸਹਸ ਸਿਆਣਪਾ ਲਖ ਹੋਹਿ ਤ ਇਕ ਨ ਚਲੈ ਨਾਲਿ॥

ਕਿਵ ਸਚਿਆਰਾ ਹੋਈਐ ਕਿਵ ਕੂੜੈ ਤੁਟੈ ਪਾਲਿ॥

ਹੁਕਮਿ ਰਜਾਈ ਚਲਣਾ ਨਾਨਕ ਲਿਖਿਆ ਨਾਲਿ॥੧॥

stanza 1

IN THE OPENING STANZA GURU NANAK DISCUSSES THE ways practiced to attain realization and rejects them one by one. Finally, he himself gives a clue to realize Truth.

Neither a hundred thousand purifications of body, nor deep and long meditations, nor any amount of worldly achievements, nor any number of mental deliberations are of any avail to realize Truth. [Guru Nanak therefore, poses the questions:] How shall we rend the veil of falsehood, and realize Truth? [He himself supplies the answer:] By accepting the Will of God pronounced for every one of us.

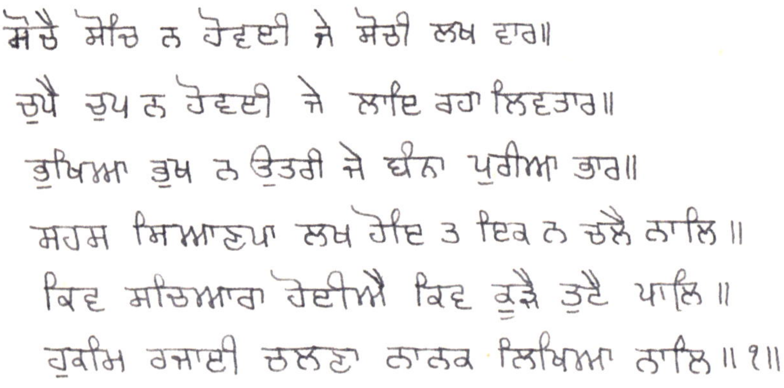

ਸੋਚੈ ਸੋਚਿ ਨ ਹੋਵਈ ਜੇ ਸੋਚੀ ਲਖ ਵਾਰ॥

ਚੁਪੈ ਚੁਪ ਨ ਹੋਵਈ ਜੇ ਲਾਇ ਰਹਾ ਲਿਵਤਾਰ॥

ਭੁਖਿਆ ਭੁਖ ਨ ਉਤਰੀ ਜੇ ਬੰਨਾ ਪੁਰੀਆ ਭਾਰ॥

ਸਹਸ ਸਿਆਣਪਾ ਲਖ ਹੋਹਿ ਤ ਇਕ ਨ ਚਲੈ ਨਾਲਿ॥

ਕਿਵ ਸਚਿਆਰਾ ਹੋਈਐ ਕਿਵ ਕੂੜੈ ਤੁਟੈ ਪਾਲਿ॥

ਹੁਕਮਿ ਰਜਾਈ ਚਲਣਾ ਨਾਨਕ ਲਿਖਿਆ ਨਾਲਿ॥੧॥

Figure 5: Original handwritten Stanza 1 by Mrs. Pushpa Bakshi.

Stanza 1

In the opening stanza Guru Nanak discusses the ways
practised to attain realization, and rejects them one by one.
Finally, he himself gives clue to realize Truth.

The Text:-

Neither a hundred thousand purifications of body, nor

deep and long meditation, nor any amount of worldly achievements,

nor any number of mental deliberations are of any avail to

realize Truth. (Guru Nanak, therefore, poses the question) How

shall we rend the veil of falsehood, and realise Truth? (He

himself supplies the answer) By accepting the Will of God

pronounced for everyone of us.

Figure 6: Original typewritten page of translation typed by
Mr. Om Prakash Bakshi.

ਹੁਕਮੀ ਹੋਵਨਿ ਆਕਾਰ ਹੁਕਮੁ ਨ ਕਹਿਆ ਜਾਈ॥

ਹੁਕਮੀ ਹੋਵਨਿ ਜੀਅ ਹੁਕਮਿ ਮਿਲੈ ਵਡਿਆਈ॥

ਹੁਕਮੀ ਉਤਮੁ ਨੀਚੁ ਹੁਕਮਿ ਲਿਖਿ ਦੁਖ ਸੁਖ ਪਾਈਅਹਿ॥

ਇਕਨਾ ਹੁਕਮੀ ਬਖਸੀਸ ਇਕਿ ਹੁਕਮੀ ਸਦਾ ਭਵਾ- ਈਅਹਿ॥

ਹੁਕਮੈ ਅੰਦਰਿ ਸਭੁ ਕੋ ਬਾਹਰਿ ਹੁਕਮ ਨ ਕੋਇ॥

ਨਾਨਕ ਹੁਕਮੈ ਜੇ ਬੁਝੈ ਤ ਹਉਮੈ ਕਹੈ ਨ ਕੋਇ॥੨॥

stanza 2

In this stanza, Guru Nanak elucidates the Will of God.

His will is not capable of (complete) description. It is by this Will that all things take shape, all living creatures are born, and all honors are conferred. It is by this will that some are rendered low and some high. Again, it is according to the dictates of this Will that we undergo sufferings and enjoyment; some receive His Grace (Moksha) while others enter the cycle of transmigration. Nothing is outside the purview of His Will. If this fact is brought home to us, we will cease to assert the independence of our own self.

ਗਾਵੈ ਕੋ ਤਾਣੁ ਹੋਵੈ ਕਿਸੈ ਤਾਣੁ॥

ਗਾਵੈ ਕੋ ਦਾਤਿ ਜਾਣੈ ਨੀਸਾਣੁ॥

ਗਾਵੈ ਕੋ ਗੁਣ ਵਡਿਆਈਆ ਚਾਰ॥

ਗਾਵੈ ਕੋ ਵਿਦਿਆ ਵਿਖਮੁ ਵੀਚਾਰੁ॥

ਗਾਵੈ ਕੋ ਸਾਜਿ ਕਰੇ ਤਨੁ ਖੇਹ॥

ਗਾਵੈ ਕੋ ਜੀਅ ਲੈ ਫਿਰਿ ਦੇਹ॥

ਗਾਵੈ ਕੋ ਜਾਪੈ ਦਿਸੈ ਦੂਰਿ॥

ਗਾਵੈ ਕੋ ਵੇਖੈ ਹਾਦਰਾ ਹਦੂਰਿ॥

ਕਥਨਾ ਕਥੀ ਨ ਆਵੈ ਤੋਟਿ॥

ਕਥਿ ਕਥਿ ਕਥੀ ਕੋਟੀ ਕੋਟਿ ਕੋਟਿ॥

ਦੇਦਾ ਦੇ ਲੈਦੇ ਥਕਿ ਪਾਹਿ॥

ਜੁਗਾ ਜੁਗੰਤਰਿ ਖਾਹੀ ਖਾਹਿ॥

ਹੁਕਮੀ ਹੁਕਮੁ ਚਲਾਏ ਰਾਹੁ॥

ਨਾਨਕ ਵਿਗਸੈ ਵੇਪਰਵਾਹੁ॥੩॥

stanza 3

Here Guru Nanak talks of the various descriptions of God the Almighty by various persons and states that it is impossible to render complete description of Him. Guru Nanak himself describes God the Almighty as the Bestower of all bounties and as One Who runs the affairs of the whole world through His ordain without feeling the least strain for it.

Some sing His praise endowed with the power to do so. Some sing His bounties symbolizing Him as the Giver of bounties. Some sing His beautiful qualities and His Greatness. Some discuss His intricate philosophy on the basis of their learnings. Some sing Him as One who adorns our bodies, and then brings them to dust. Some sing Him as One Who takes our lives, and again brings us back to life. Some sing Him as One Who is seeing us all being omnipresent. Millions of persons have described Him in millions of ways, but still His description remains incomplete. [Guru Nanak himself adds:] The Almighty is showering His blessings on the receivers endlessly to the extent that the receivers get weary of receiving. They have been thriving on His bounties through all ages. The Almighty by His ordination is running the affairs of the universe, Himself feeling carefree.

ਸਾਚਾ ਸਾਹਿਬੁ ਸਾਚੁ ਨਾਇ ਭਾਖਿਆ ਭਾਉ ਅਪਾਰੁ॥

ਆਖਹਿ ਮੰਗਹਿ ਦੇਹਿ ਦੇਹਿ ਦਾਤਿ ਕਰੇ ਦਾਤਾਰੁ॥

ਫੇਰਿ ਕਿ ਅਗੈ ਰਖੀਐ ਜਿਤੁ ਦਿਸੈ ਦਰਬਾਰੁ॥

ਮੁਹੌ ਕਿ ਬੋਲਣੁ ਬੋਲੀਐ ਜਿਤੁ ਸੁਣਿ ਧਰੇ ਪਿਆਰੁ॥

ਅੰਮ੍ਰਿਤ ਵੇਲਾ ਸਚੁ ਨਾਉ ਵਡਿਆਈ ਵੀਚਾਰੁ॥

ਕਰਮੀ ਆਵੈ ਕਪੜਾ ਨਦਰੀ ਮੋਖੁ ਦੁਆਰੁ॥

ਨਾਨਕ ਏਵੈ ਜਾਣੀਐ ਸਭੁ ਆਪੇ ਸਚਿਆਰੁ॥੪॥

stanza 4

IN THIS STANZA GURU NANAK EXPLAINS HOW TO HAVE AN access to God the Almighty and attain *nirvana*. Guru Nanak believes in *"Karma-theory"* but points out that good actions alone will not enable us to attain *nirvana*. For that, asserts Guru Nanak, we have to earn Grace of God the Almighty by our utter surrender to Him, accepting Him as all in all.

> The Almighty is True and true are His ways. Infinite love is His language. We beg of Him for favors and He continues obliging. What offerings should, then, we take with us to seek access to Him? What, then, should we utter from our lips hearing which He may love us? [Guru Nanak answers:] In the early hours of morning meditate on His greatness, for birth is shaped according to our deeds, but nirvana can be had only through His Grace. By doing so, O Nanak[1], the realization that the Almighty is all-in-all shall dawn on us.

---

[1] Here and in subsequent stanzas, Guru Nanak addresses himself as "O Nanak" for emphasis.

ਥਾਪਿਆ ਨ ਜਾਇ ਕੀਤਾ ਨ ਹੋਇ॥

ਆਪੇ ਆਪਿ ਨਿਰੰਜਨੁ ਸੋਇ॥

ਜਿਨਿ ਸੇਵਿਆ ਤਿਨਿ ਪਾਇਆ ਮਾਨੁ॥

ਨਾਨਕ ਗਾਵੀਐ ਗੁਣੀ ਨਿਧਾਨੁ॥

ਗਾਵੀਐ ਸੁਣੀਐ ਮਨਿ ਰਖੀਐ ਭਾਉ॥

ਦੁਖੁ ਪਰਹਰਿ ਸੁਖੁ ਘਰਿ ਲੈ ਜਾਇ॥

ਗੁਰਮੁਖਿ ਨਾਦੰ ਗੁਰਮੁਖਿ ਵੇਦੰ ਗੁਰਮੁਖਿ ਰਹਿਆ ਸਮਾਈ॥

ਗੁਰੁ ਈਸਰੁ ਗੁਰੁ ਗੋਰਖੁ ਬਰਮਾ ਗੁਰੁ ਪਾਰਬਤੀ ਮਾਈ॥

ਜੇ ਹਉ ਜਾਣਾ ਆਖਾ ਨਾਹੀ ਕਹਣਾ ਕਥਨੁ ਨ ਜਾਈ॥

ਗੁਰਾ ਇਕ ਦੇਹਿ ਬੁਝਾਈ॥

ਸਭਨਾ ਜੀਆ ਕਾ ਇਕੁ ਦਾਤਾ ਸੋ ਮੈ ਵਿਸਰਿ ਨ ਜਾਈ॥੫॥

ﾅﾐﾝﾃﾞﾝﾝﾝ 5

HERE GURU NANAK FURTHER ADORNS GOD THE ALMIGHTY. He then talks about the power of *guru* through whom contact can be had to God the Almighty whom Guru Nanak would not like to forget even for a moment.

God the Almighty cannot be made and shaped in any material form. He is beyond all material-ism, and exists solely by Himself. His existence is manifested to those who seek after Him. O Nanak, sing praises of God the Almighty—the treasure of all excellences. Let us sing and hear His praises, and keep love for Him in our hearts. By our doing so He will take us from the world of pain and suffering to the world of joy and bliss. Guru's words, inspired as they are by God Him-self, are the words of Nada. Guru is god Shiva, god Vishnu, and god Brahma. He is goddess Par-bati and goddess Lakshmi. Even if I knew the power of guru, I would not attempt to describe it, for it is not capable of description. O Guru, drive home to me one thing: That I never forget God the Almighty, the sole benefactor of all humanity.

੧ਓ

ਸਾਹਿਬੁ ਕਲਿ ਜੁਗੁ ਭੂਮੀ
ਬਹੁਰਿ ਦੇਖੁ ਕਲ ਜੁਗ
ਤੈ ਗੁਨੀ ਵੇਰੁ ਖੂਸ
ਦੀਆ ॥ ਰਾਜੁ ਪੁਨ ॥੨॥

ਆਦਿ ਪਰਮੇਸੁਰ ਜੁਗਾਦਿ ਜੁਗੀ ॥   ੴ ਸ੍ਰੀ ਗੁਰੂ ਗ੍ਰੰਥ ਜੀ ਕੀ ਪੋਥੀ ॥

Figure 8: Mural of Guru Nanak presenting and chanting the Japuji Sahib in the presence of Guru Angad with Bhai Bala to side with a fly-whisk, circa 19th century. The Mul Mantar is inscribed to the left.

Figure 7 (left): Folio of the Japuji Sahib from the Kartarpur Bir, penned by Bhai Gurdas. This manuscript was formally installed in the Golden Temple complex in 1604. The Kartarpur Bir is currently preserved by the Sodhi descendants of Dhir Mal in the village of Kartarpur, located in the Jalandhar district of Punjab, India. A rare and sacred treasure, the manuscript is publicly displayed only once a year—on the day of Vaisakhi (also spelled Baisakhi), one of the most important festivals in the Sikh calendar.

ਤੀਰਥਿ ਨਾਵਾ ਜੇ ਤਿਸੁ ਭਾਵਾ ਵਿਣੁ ਭਾਣੇ ਕਿ ਨਾਇ ਕਰੀ॥

ਜੇਤੀ ਸਿਰਠਿ ਉਪਾਈ ਵੇਖਾ ਵਿਣੁ ਕਰਮਾ ਕਿ ਮਿਲੈ ਲਈ॥

ਮਤਿ ਵਿਚਿ ਰਤਨ ਜਵਾਹਰ ਮਾਣਿਕ ਜੇ ਇੱਕ ਗੁਰ ਕੀ ਸਿਖ ਸੁਣੀ॥

ਗੁਰਾ ਇਕ ਦੇਹਿ ਬੁਝਾਈ॥

ਸਭਨਾ ਜੀਆ ਕਾ ਇਕੁ ਦਾਤਾ ਸੋ ਮੈ ਵਿਸਰਿ ਨ ਜਾਈ॥੬॥

stanza 6

GURU NANAK, IN THIS STANZA, TALKS OF THE EFFICACY OF the Divine Will and instrumentality of *guru* to realize Truth.

I would take holy dips at sacred Places, only if by doing so I could please Him. Otherwise, what was the use of it? Whatever creation I see in this world cannot get anything without His Grace. Many precious gems and jewels lie hidden in man's soul, but they come to surface, only if we listen to the advice of guru. O Guru, drive home to me one thing: That I never forget the sole benefactor of humanity.

ਜੇ ਜੁਗ ਚਾਰੇ ਆਰਜਾ ਹੋਰ ਦਸੂਣੀ ਹੋਇ॥

ਨਵਾ ਖੰਡਾ ਵਿਚਿ ਜਾਣੀਐ ਨਾਲਿ ਚਲੈ ਸਭੁ ਕੋਇ॥

ਚੰਗਾ ਨਾਉ ਰਖਾਇ ਕੈ ਜਸੁ ਕੀਰਤਿ ਜਗਿ ਲੇਇ॥

ਜੇ ਤਿਸੁ ਨਦਰਿ ਨ ਆਵਈ ਤ ਵਾਤ ਨ ਪੁਛੈ ਕੇ॥

ਕੀਟਾ ਅੰਦਰਿ ਕੀਟੁ ਕਰਿ ਦੋਸੀ ਦੋਸੁ ਧਰੇ॥

ਨਾਨਕ ਨਿਰਗੁਣਿ ਗੁਣੁ ਕਰੇ ਗੁਣਵੰਤਿਆ ਗੁਣੁ
ਦੇ॥

ਤੇਹਾ ਕੋਇ ਨ ਸੁਝਈ ਜਿ ਤਿਸੁ ਗੁਣੁ ਕੋਇ
ਕਰੇ॥੭॥

स्tanza 7

G‌URU N‌ANAK ONCE MORE STRESSES, IN THIS STANZA, THAT nothing good or great can be achieved without the Divine Will.

If a man's life were four ages long, and even ten times more than it; if he were known in all the continents of the world, and all people were to follow him; if he were to earn a good name and win all the honor and praise of the world, it would be of little account without receiving His Grace. In the eyes of God he would be held as a culprit, and graded as the meanest of insects. O Nanak, God the Almighty bestows excellence on those who are without any excellence, and adds to the excellences of those who have them. But I find no one who can do any good to God in return.

ਸੁਣਿਐ ਸਿਧ ਪੀਰ ਸੁਰਿ ਨਾਥ॥
ਸੁਣਿਐ ਧਰਤਿ ਧਵਲ ਆਕਾਸ॥
ਸੁਣਿਐ ਦੀਪ ਲੋਅ ਪਾਤਾਲ॥
ਸੁਣਿਐ ਪੋਹਿ ਨ ਸਕੈ ਕਾਲੁ॥
ਨਾਨਕ ਭਗਤਾ ਸਦਾ ਵਿਗਾਸੁ॥
ਸੁਣਿਐ ਦੂਖ ਪਾਪ ਕਾ ਨਾਸੁ॥੮॥

stanza 8

IN STANZAS 8 TO 11, GURU NANAK DESCRIBES THE ATTAIN-
ment of one who listens to the inner voice which emanates
from God the Almighty—the source of all consciousness—
and transcends to lower regions. This voice has been heard
by different saints of different ages and has been referred to
by them by various names, viz. "Music of spheres," "*Baange
Ajab*," "*Baange Ilahi*," "Naad," etc. Guru Nanak calls it *Naam*.

By listening to Naam one attains the status of
Sidhas, Pirs, Sura and Nathas—the elevated
souls. One comes to know of the real nature of
earth, the supporting bull, the sky, the islands, the
underworlds, and the spheres. Again, by listening to Naam one attains immortality, and one's
sorrows and sins are brought to an end. The devotees who listens to Naam are always happy and
ever-fragrant.

ਸੁਣਿਐ ਈਸਰੁ ਬਰਮਾ ਇੰਦੁ॥

ਸੁਣਿਐ ਮੁਖਿ ਸਾਲਾਹਣ ਮੰਦੁ॥

ਸੁਣਿਐ ਜੋਗ ਜੁਗਤਿ ਤਨਿ ਭੇਦ॥

ਸੁਣਿਐ ਸਾਸਤ ਸਿਮ੍ਰਿਤਿ ਵੇਦ॥

ਨਾਨਕ ਭਗਤਾ ਸਦਾ ਵਿਗਾਸੁ॥

ਸੁਣਿਐ ਦੂਖ ਪਾਪ ਕਾ ਨਾਸੁ॥੯॥

stanza 9

By listening to Naam one attains the status of
Shiva, Brahma, and Indra. Even wicked people
begin to sing His praise by listening to Naam.
By listening to Naam one comes to know how to
have an access to Him, while encased in this body.
By listening to Naam one attains the ever fragrant
state transcending all the sins and sorrows.

ਸੁਣਿਐ ਸਤੁ ਸੰਤੋਖੁ ਗਿਆਨੁ ॥
ਸੁਣਿਐ ਅਠਸਠਿ ਕਾ ਇਸਨਾਨੁ ॥
ਸੁਣਿਐ ਪੜਿ ਪੜਿ ਪਾਵਹਿ ਮਾਨੁ ॥
ਸੁਣਿਐ ਲਾਗੈ ਸਹਜਿ ਧਿਆਨੁ ॥
ਨਾਨਕ ਭਗਤਾ ਸਦਾ ਵਿਗਾਸੁ ॥
ਸੁਣਿਐ ਦੂਖ ਪਾਪ ਕਾ ਨਾਸੁ ॥੧੦॥

stanza 10

By listening to Naam one acquires truth, contentment and knowledge, the good effect had by bathing at sixty-eight places of pilgrimage, the respect earned after devoted years of study, steady and easy concentration in meditation. By listening to Naam one attains the ever-fragrant state transcending all the sins and sorrows.

ਸੁਣਿਐ ਸਰਾ ਗੁਣਾ ਕੇ ਗਾਹ ॥
ਸੁਣਿਐ ਸੇਖ ਪੀਰ ਪਾਤਿਸਾਹ ॥
ਸੁਣਿਐ ਅੰਧੇ ਪਾਵਹਿ ਰਾਹੁ ॥
ਸੁਣਿਐ ਹਾਥ ਹੋਵੈ ਅਸਗਾਹੁ ॥
ਨਾਨਕ ਭਗਤਾ ਸਦਾ ਵਿਗਾਸੁ ॥
ਸੁਣਿਐ ਦੂਖ ਪਾਪ ਕਾ ਨਾਸੁ ॥੧੧॥

stanza 11

By listening to Naam one acquires all the virtues, and attains the highest status in the worldly as well as spiritual fields. By listening to Naam a novice finds the path of access to higher regions for realization of God. By listening to Naam one fathoms the mysteries of the world. By listening to Naam one attains the ever-fragrant state transcending all the sins and sorrows.

ਮੰਨੇ ਕੀ ਗਤਿ ਕਹੀ ਨ ਜਾਇ॥

ਜੇ ਕੋ ਕਹੈ ਪਿਛੈ ਪਛੁਤਾਇ॥

ਕਾਗਦਿ ਕਲਮ ਨ ਲਿਖਣਹਾਰੁ॥

ਮੰਨੇ ਕਾ ਬਹਿ ਕਰਨਿ ਵੀਚਾਰੁ॥

ਐਸਾ ਨਾਮੁ ਨਿਰੰਜਨੁ ਹੋਇ॥

ਜੇ ਕੋ ਮੰਨਿ ਜਾਣੈ ਮਨਿ ਕੋਇ॥੧੨॥

ङ्तanza 12

In stanzas 12 to 15, Guru Nanak describes the condi-tion of believer. In common parlance one who believes in the existence of God is a believer, and one who does not believe in the existence of God is a non-believer or atheist. But, in fact, both are non-believers insofar as neither has seen God. "God Himself is Formless, but He assumed Form. He became the *Word* or *Naam*. It was from this Word that the various planes of creation sprang into existence, one below the other."[2]

By the word *believer,* Guru Nanak means: "He who practic-es the *Word,* i.e. withdraws his soul from the body and lets it be drawn up by the power of the *Divine Music* of the *Word* from one spiritual plane to another, until he reaches the very source and becomes one with it."[3]

> The blessed state of the person who has estab-lished contact with Naam cannot he described. Whosoever endeavors to describe it has to repent afterwards. No writer can describe it in writing, no amount of deliberations of assembly of wise persons can comprehend it. So immaculate is Naam. But rare are the persons who know it.

---

[2] From *The Japuji* by Sant Kirpal Singh, published by Ruhani Satsang, Sawan Ashram, Delhi-7 (p. 97)
[3] Ibid.

37

ਮੰਨੈ ਸੁਰਤਿ ਹੋਵੈ ਮਨਿ ਬੁਧਿ॥
ਮੰਨੈ ਸਗਲ ਭਵਣ ਕੀ ਸੁਧਿ॥
ਮੰਨੈ ਮੁਹਿ ਚੋਟਾ ਨਾ ਖਾਇ॥
ਮੰਨੈ ਜਮ ਕੈ ਸਾਥਿ ਨ ਜਾਇ॥
ਐਸਾ ਨਾਮੁ ਨਿਰੰਜਨੁ ਹੋਇ॥
ਜੇ ਕੋ ਮੰਨਿ ਜਾਣੈ ਮਨਿ ਕੋਇ॥੧੩॥

stanza 13

The contact with Naam awakens the mind and intellect to a higher state of consciousness. The person who has established contact with Naam acquires knowledge of all the spheres of life. Such a person tastes no defeat. Even the fear of death is no longer a fear for him. So immaculate is Naam. But rare are the persons who know it.

ਮੰਨੈ ਮਾਰਗਿ ਠਾਕ ਨ ਪਾਇ॥
ਮੰਨੈ ਪਤਿ ਸਿਉ ਪਰਗਟੁ ਜਾਇ॥
ਮੰਨੈ ਮਗੁ ਨ ਚਲੈ ਪੰਥੁ॥
ਮੰਨੈ ਧਰਮ ਸੇਤੀ ਸਨਬੰਧੁ॥
ਐਸਾ ਨਾਮੁ ਨਿਰੰਜਨੁ ਹੋਇ॥
ਜੇ ਕੋ ਮੰਨਿ ਜਾਣੈ ਮਨਿ ਕੋਇ॥੧੪॥

stanza 14

The person who has established contact with Naam has smooth sailing in life, and he completes this earthly sojourn successfully and honorably. Such a person being in direct contact with truth has neither to tread the way to hell nor that to heaven. So immaculate is Naam. But rare are the persons who know it.

ਮੰਨੈ ਪਾਵਹਿ ਮੋਖੁ ਦੁਆਰੁ॥
ਮੰਨੈ ਪਰਵਾਰੈ ਸਾਧਾਰੁ॥
ਮੰਨੈ ਤਰੈ ਤਾਰੇ ਗੁਰੁਸਿਖ॥
ਮੰਨੈ ਨਾਨਕ ਭਵਹਿ ਨ ਭਿਖ॥
ਐਸਾ ਨਾਮੁ ਨਿਰੰਜਨੁ ਹੋਇ॥
ਜੇ ਕੋ ਮੰਨਿ ਜਾਣੈ ਮਨਿ ਕੋਇ॥ ੧੫॥

stanza 15

The person who has established contact with Naam finds the door to salvation. His kith and kin also secure the spiritual support of Naam. The spiritual teacher achieves salvation through Naam, and takes out his disciples from the cycle of transmigration through this very power of Naam. The person who has established contact with Naam does not go abegging. So immaculate is Naam. But rare are the persons who know it.

ੴ ਸਤਿਨਾਮੁ ਕਰਤਾ ਪੁਰਖੁ
ਨਿਰਭਉ ਨਿਰਵੈਰੁ ਅਕਾਲ ਮੂਰਤਿ ਅਜੂਨੀ
ਸੈਭੰ ਗੁਰ ਪ੍ਰਸਾਦਿ

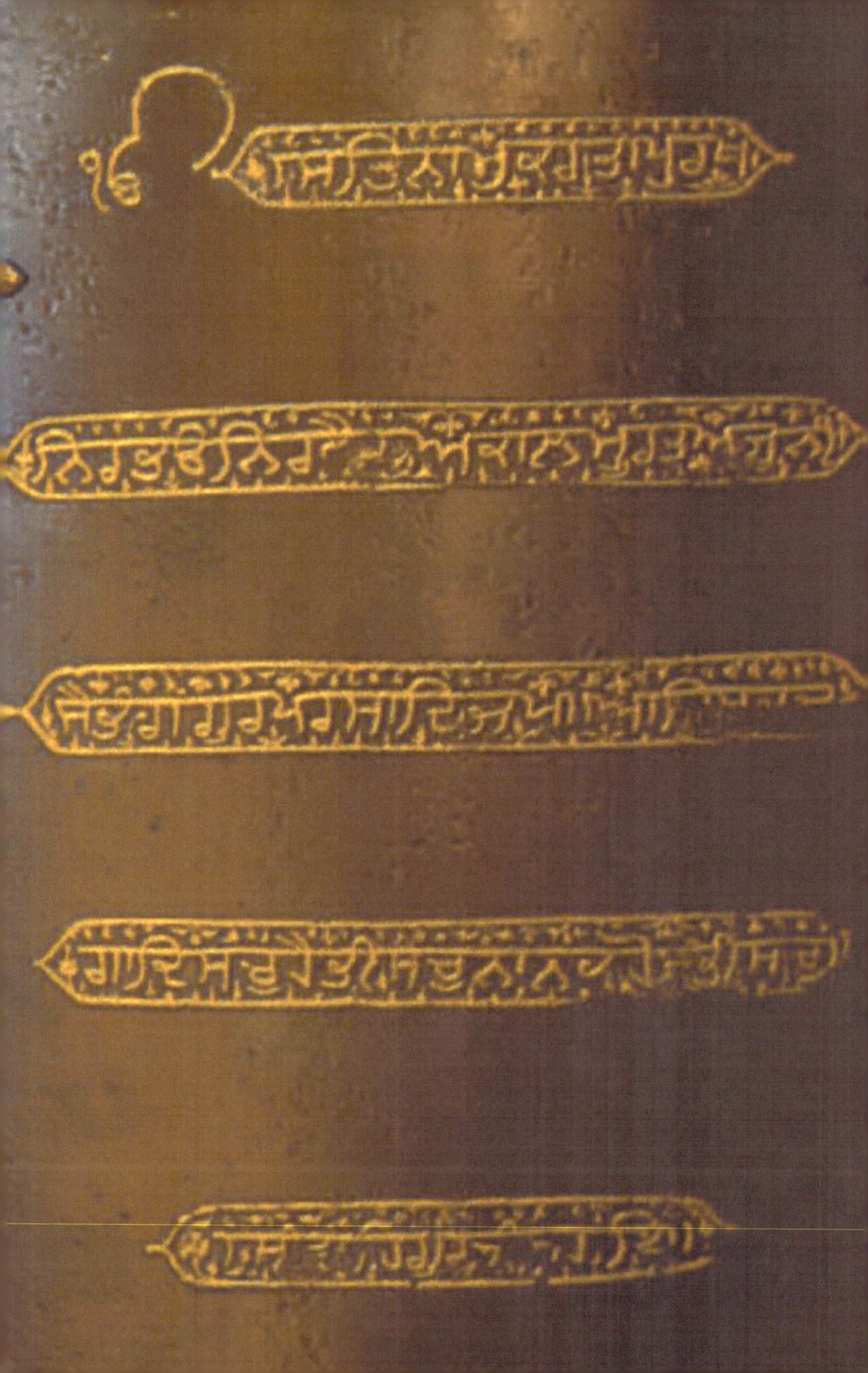

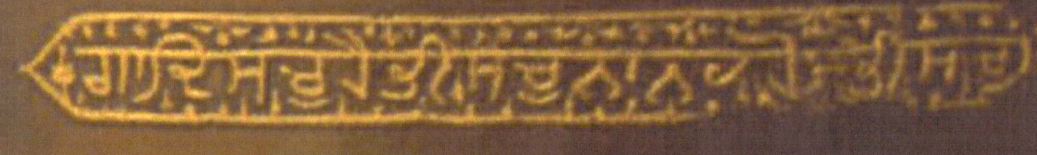

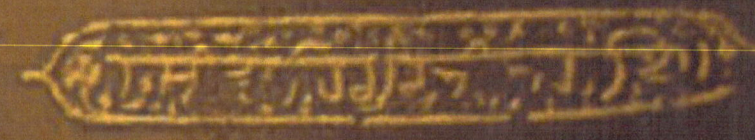

Figure 10: Illuminated Adi Granth folio with nisan of Guru Gobind Singh. Lahore recension, late 17th to early 18th century. Collection of Takht Sri Harimandir Sahib, Patna.

Figure 9 (left): Opening verses of the Japuji Sahib composition of Guru Nanak inscribed on a plate of the 'Charaina' body armour containing verses from the Guru Granth Sahib and Dasam Granth inscribed on each plate. The armor was worn by Guru Gobind Singh in the battle of Bhangani, ca.1688. Collection of the royal family of the former state of Patiala. Author unknown.

ਪੰਚ ਪਰਵਾਣ ਪੰਚ ਪਰਧਾਨੁ॥

ਪੰਚੇ ਪਾਵਹਿ ਦਰਗਹਿ ਮਾਨੁ॥

ਪੰਚੇ ਸੋਹਹਿ ਦਰਿ ਰਾਜਾਨੁ॥

ਪੰਚਾ ਕਾ ਗੁਰੁ ਏਕੁ ਧਿਆਨੁ॥

ਜੇ ਕੋ ਕਹੈ ਕਰੈ ਵੀਚਾਰੁ॥

ਕਰਤੇ ਕੈ ਕਰਣੈ ਨਾਹੀ ਸੁਮਾਰੁ॥

ਧੌਲੁ ਧਰਮੁ ਦਇਆ ਕਾ ਪੂਤੁ॥

ਸੰਤੋਖੁ ਥਾਪਿ ਰਖਿਆ ਜਿਨਿ ਸੂਤਿ॥

ਜੇ ਕੋ ਬੁਝੈ ਹੋਵੈ ਸਚਿਆਰੁ॥

ਧਵਲੈ ਉਪਰਿ ਕੇਤਾ ਭਾਰੁ॥

ਧਰਤੀ ਹੋਰੁ ਪਰੈ ਹੋਰੁ ਹੋਰੁ॥

ਤਿਸ ਤੇ ਭਾਰੁ ਤਲੈ ਕਵਣੁ ਜੋਰੁ॥

stanza 16

In this stanza, Guru Nanak talks of the power of *Naam* or *Word*. It is from this *Word* that the whole world came into being. Guru Nanak concludes that it is beyond the power of anyone to describe the power of *Naam*.

Such persons who listen to Naam and have contact with it are panchs—the chieftains. They are valued in God's estimation and are accepted by Him. They grace His council as kings. The sole guide of such reasons is the constant thought of God. If someone were to describe and ponder over the mysteries of Nature, he would not reach any conclusion, for fathomless are the mysteries of Nature.

The fabled bull supporting the earth is the law of God the Almighty running this universe. This law born out of His mercy is binding the whole system in harmony. Whosoever knows this truth would have the realization dawn on him. Otherwise how can such a load of earth be lifted by the fabled bull? Again, there are earths underneath this earth, and who is supporting the last earth?

(continued on next page)

ਜੀਅ ਜਾਤਿ ਰੰਗਾ ਕੇ ਨਾਵ॥

ਸਭਨਾ ਲਿਖਿਆ ਵੁੜੀ ਕਲਾਮ॥

ਏਹੁ ਲੇਖਾ ਲਿਖਿ ਜਾਣੈ ਕੋਇ॥

ਲੇਖਾ ਲਿਖਿਆ ਕੇਤਾ ਹੋਇ॥

ਕੇਤਾ ਤਾਣੁ ਸੁਆਲਿਹੁ ਰੂਪੁ॥

ਕੇਤੀ ਦਾਤਿ ਜਾਣੈ ਕੌਣੁ ਕੂਤੁ॥

ਕੀਤਾ ਪਸਾਉ ਏਕੋ ਕਵਾਉ॥

ਤਿਸ ਤੇ ਹੋਏ ਲਖ ਦਰੀਆਉ॥

ਕੁਦਰਤਿ ਕਵਣ ਕਹਾ ਵੀਚਾਰੁ॥

ਵਾਰਿਆ ਨ ਜਾਵਾ ਏਕ ਵਾਰ॥

ਜੋ ਤੁਧੁ ਭਾਵੈ ਸਾਈ ਭਲੀ ਕਾਰ॥

ਤੂ ਸਦਾ ਸਲਾਮਤਿ ਨਿਰੰਕਾਰ॥ ੧੯॥

The countless creatures of different species and colors have been recorded by the ever-flowing pen of God. Who else can keep such a record, and how long would it take? How great is His might, how charming is His beauty, and how great are His bounties—who can estimate? With His one word the whole world came into being, and hundreds of thousands of rivers began to flow. What power have I to describe and contemplate Thee? I cannot even once admire Thee completely. Whatever pleaseth Thee is the only good deed—O Formless, and the Only Immortal One.

ਅਸੰਖ ਜਪ ਅਸੰਖ ਭਾਉ ॥

ਅਸੰਖ ਪੂਜਾ ਅਸੰਖ ਤਪ ਤਾਉ ॥

ਅਸੰਖ ਗਰੰਥ ਮੁਖਿ ਵੇਦ ਪਾਠ ॥

ਅਸੰਖ ਜੋਗ ਮਨਿ ਰਹਹਿ ਉਦਾਸ ॥

ਅਸੰਖ ਭਗਤ ਗੁਣ ਗਿਆਨ ਵੀਚਾਰ ॥

ਅਸੰਖ ਸਤੀ ਅਸੰਖ ਦਾਤਾਰ ॥

ਅਸੰਖ ਸੂਰ ਮੁਹ ਭਖ ਸਾਰ ॥

ਅਸੰਖ ਮੋਨਿ ਲਿਵ ਲਾਇ ਤਾਰ ॥

ਕੁਦਰਤਿ ਕਵਣ ਕਹਾ ਵੀਚਾਰੁ ॥

ਵਾਰਿਆ ਨ ਜਾਵਾ ਏਕ ਵਾਰ ॥

ਜੋ ਤੁਧੁ ਭਾਵੈ ਸਾਈ ਭਲੀ ਕਾਰ ॥

ਤੂ ਸਦਾ ਸਲਾਮਤਿ ਨਿਰੰਕਾਰ ॥ ੧੭ ॥

stanza 17

IN STANZAS 17 & 18, GURU NANAK ASSERTS THE DIVERSITY of this world. There are innumerable sorts of pious and impious persons inhabiting this world. Guru Nanak lists these pious and impious persons in these two stanzas.

There is no count of those who constantly utter Thy name nor of those who adore Thee. There is no count of those who worship Thee, nor of those who are engaged in asceticism. There is no count of those who are reciting the holy texts and vedas verbatim, nor of those who are engaged in yoga, and feel detached. There is no count of devotees who ponder over Thy virtues, nor of those who are virtuous and benevolent. There is no count of warriors who boldly face the steel, nor of the mute worshipers immersed in meditation.

What Power have I to describe and contemplate Thee? I cannot even once admire Thee completely. Whatever pleaseth Thee is the only good deed—O Formless and the Only Immortal One.

ਅਸੰਖ ਮੂਰਖ ਅੰਧ ਘੋਰ॥

ਅਸੰਖ ਚੋਰ ਹਰਾਮਖੋਰ॥

ਅਸੰਖ ਅਮਰ ਕਰਿ ਜਾਹਿ ਜੋਰ॥

ਅਸੰਖ ਗਲ ਵਢ ਹਤਿਆ ਕਮਾਹਿ॥

ਅਸੰਖ ਪਾਪੀ ਪਾਪੁ ਕਰਿ ਜਾਹਿ॥

ਅਸੰਖ ਕੂੜਿਆਰ ਕੂੜੇ ਫਿਰਾਹਿ॥

ਅਸੰਖ ਮਲੇਛ ਮਲੁ ਭਖਿ ਖਾਹਿ॥

ਅਸੰਖ ਨਿੰਦਕ ਸਿਰਿ ਕਰਹਿ ਭਾਰੁ॥

ਨਾਨਕੁ ਨੀਚੁ ਕਹੈ ਵੀਚਾਰੁ॥

ਵਾਰਿਆ ਨ ਜਾਵਾ ਏਕ ਵਾਰ॥

ਜੋ ਤੁਧੁ ਭਾਵੈ ਸਾਈ ਭਲੀ ਕਾਰ॥

ਤੂ ਸਦਾ ਸਲਾਮਤਿ ਨਿਰੰਕਾਰ॥ ੧੮॥

stanza 18

There is no count of fools of the first order; nor of thieves who thrive on another's property. There is no count of tyrants exercising tyranny by their despotic orders and excesses, nor of those whose hands are soiled with blood of men. There is no count of sinners who depart from here committing sins, nor of the liars all lost in telling lies. There is no count of the filthy people living on filth, nor of the slanderers. Thus thinks Nanak, the lowly.

I cannot even once admire Thee completely. Whatever pleaseth Thee is the only good deed—O Formless and the Only Immortal One.

ਅਸੰਖ ਨਾਵ ਅਸੰਖ ਥਾਵ॥

ਅਗੰਮ ਅਗੰਮ ਅਸੰਖ ਲੋਅ॥

ਅਸੰਖ ਕਹਹਿ ਸਿਰਿ ਭਾਰੁ ਹੋਇ॥

ਅਖਰੀ ਨਾਮੁ ਅਖਰੀ ਸਾਲਾਹ॥

ਅਖਰੀ ਗਿਆਨੁ ਗੀਤ ਗੁਣ ਗਾਹ॥

ਅਖਰੀ ਲਿਖਣੁ ਬੋਲਣੁ ਬਾਣਿ॥

ਅਖਰਾ ਸਿਰਿ ਸੰਜੋਗੁ ਵਖਾਣਿ॥

ਜਿਨਿ ਏਹਿ ਲਿਖੇ ਤਿਸੁ ਸਿਰਿ ਨਾਹਿ॥

ਜਿਵ ਫੁਰਮਾਏ ਤਿਵ ਤਿਵ ਪਾਹਿ॥

ਜੇਤਾ ਕੀਤਾ ਤੇਤਾ ਨਾਉ॥

ਵਿਣੁ ਨਾਵੈ ਨਾਹੀ ਕੋ ਥਾਉ॥

ਕੁਦਰਤਿ ਕਵਣ ਕਹਾ ਵੀਚਾਰੁ॥

ਵਾਰਿਆ ਨ ਜਾਵਾ ਏਕ ਵਾਰ॥

ਜੋ ਤੁਧੁ ਭਾਵੈ ਸਾਈ ਭਲੀ ਕਾਰ॥

ਤੂ ਸਦਾ ਸਲਾਮਤਿ ਨਿਰੰਕਾਰ॥ ੧੯॥

स्तंजा 19

Countless are Thy names and countless Thy abodes. Countless are Thy regions inaccessible. Even to call them countless is to be guilty of low estimation. It is by words that we can know, sing, and compute Thy virtues. It is by words, again, that we can write and speak. It is by words that our destined fate can be described. But the One Who wrote this destined fate for us in words is Himself not bound by any words.

We receive what He ordains for us. Whatever has been created is through Naam. Naam is all pervading force and there is no place without it.

What power have I to describe and contemplate Thee? I cannot even once admire Thee completely. Whatever pleaseth Thee is the only good deed—O Formless and the Only Immortal One.

ਭਰੀਐ ਹਥੁ ਪੈਰੁ ਤਨੁ ਦੇਹ॥

ਪਾਣੀ ਧੋਤੈ ਉਤਰਸੁ ਖੇਹ॥

ਮੂਤ ਪਲੀਤੀ ਕਪੜੁ ਹੋਇ॥

ਦੇ ਸਾਬੂਣੁ ਲਈਐ ਓਹੁ ਧੋਇ॥

ਭਰੀਐ ਮਤਿ ਪਾਪਾ ਕੈ ਸੰਗਿ॥

ਓਹੁ ਧੋਪੈ ਨਾਵੈ ਕੈ ਰੰਗਿ॥

ਪੁੰਨੀ ਪਾਪੀ ਆਖਣੁ ਨਾਹਿ॥

ਕਰਿ ਕਰਿ ਕਰਣਾ ਲਿਖਿ ਲੈ ਜਾਹੁ॥

ਆਪੇ ਬੀਜਿ ਆਪੇ ਹੀ ਖਾਹੁ॥

ਨਾਨਕ ਹੁਕਮੀ ਆਵਹੁ ਜਾਹੁ॥ ੨੦॥

stanza 20

In this stanza, Guru Nanak talks of transmigration of soul as a result of application of *Karma Theory* and tells us that the only way to come out of this cycle is through contact with *Naam—The Holy Word.*

If we pollute our hands, feet and bodies, we wash them clean with water. If we pollute our clothes, we wash them clean with soap. If we pollute our souls with sins, we can wash them clean by Naam.

Virtuous and vicious are not simply terms of reference. Every person carries forward the sum total of his good and bad actions; and as he sows, so he is made to reap. And in this way he comes and goes by His ordain.

ੴ ਸਤਿਨਾਮੁ ਕਰਤਾਪੁਰਖੁ ਨਿਰਭਉ ਨਿਰਵੈਰੁ
ਅਕਾਲਮੂਰਤਿ ਅਜੂਨੀ ਸੈਭੰ ਗੁਰਪ੍ਰਸਾਦਿ ॥
ਸਲੋਕ ਮਹਲਾ ॥   ਪਾਤਿਪੁਸਤਕ ਸਾਖਿਆ
ਬਾਣੀ ਸਿਧਿ ਪੁਰ ਸਿ ਬਹੁ ਲ ਸਮਾਧਿ ਸਮੁ ਖਿ ਰੂ ਨੁ ਬਿ ਭੂ ਤ ਸਮੀ
ਰੈ ਪਾਲਤੈ ਲਾ ਬੀਰਗੀ ਗਾਥਿ ਮਾ ਤਿਲਕਾ ਲਿ ਲਾ ਹੀ ਹੁ ਇ ਘੇ ਰੀ
ਬਸਰ ਕ ਪਟੀ ਲੇ ਜ ਸਿ ਬ੍ਰਹਮ ਕ ਸਾ ਸ ਭ ਖ ਕਟ ਸਿ ਸੇ ਵ ਕ ਸਾ
ਰ ਹੁ ਨਾਨਕ ਸਿ ਸੇ ਪਿਰ ਦੈ ਸ਼ਿ ਤੁ ਸਤਿ ਗੁ ਰ ਬਟ ਨ ਪ ਦੈ ॥੧॥ ੴ
ਨਹ ਕਲਤ ਸਨ ਨਮ ਸ੍ਰੁ ਜਾ ਵ ਰ ਬ੍ਰ ਹ ਮ ਤਾ ਰਿ ਖ੍ਵ ਦੋ ਸਾ ਗ ਰ ਸੈ ਸ ਰੁ
ਗੁ ਰ ਪ੍ਰ ਸਾ ਦੀ ਤ ਰੀ ਇ ਕ ਰ ਦ ਕ ਰ ਸ ਮ ਜ ਭੂ ਤ ਨ ਕ ਬੀ ਰ
ਗ੍ਹਾ ਕ ਰ ਕ ਰ ਤੈ ਮੈ ਤੈ ਕੀ ਨਿ ਕ ਲ ਕ ਬੀ ਪਾ ॥ ਜ ਗ ਮ ਘ ਰ ਗੀ
ਆ ਸ ਘ ਰ ਘੇ ਰ ਸ ਘ ਰ ਭੂ ਅ ਤ ਜਾ ਸ ਰੀ ਸ ਬ ਰ ਭੂ ਸ ਸ ਬ ਰ ਭੂ ਤ
ਸ ਬ ਰ ਪੁ ਜਿ ਤ ਜਾ ਸ ਸ ਬ ਰ ਤ ਤ ਏ ਕ ਸ ਬ ਰ ਨੇ ਨੋ ਨਾ ਮਿ ਬੋ ਰੁ ॥
ਨ ਕ ਰ ਤੇ ਕੇ ਸੁ ਜੈ ਸੇ ਧੀ ਲਿ ਨ ਤ ਦੇ ਉ ॥ ੨ ॥ ਏ ਵ ਹਿ ਸੂ ਬ ਸ ਬ ਰ ਦੈ
ਵੈ ਰ ਵ ਰ ਤ ਤ ਮ ਨ ਆ ਤ ਮਾ ਸ੍ਰੀ ਬ ਮੂ ਦੇ ਵ ਸੁ ਜੋ ਕੀ ਧੀ ਜਾ ਮਿ ਬੈ ਤ
ਨ ਕ ਰ ਤੇ ਕੇ ਸੁ ਜੈ ਸੇ ਧੀ ਲਿ ਨ ਜ ਨ ਦੇ ਉ ॥ ੩ ॥

Figure 11: Guru Granth Sahib manuscript housed at Sri Keshgarh Sahib, Anandpur. Dated to 1803 B.S. (1746 C.E.).

ਤੀਰਥੁ ਤਪੁ ਦਇਆ ਦਤੁ ਦਾਨੁ॥
ਜੇ ਕੋ ਪਾਵੈ ਤਿਲ ਕਾ ਮਾਨੁ॥
ਸੁਣਿਆ ਮੰਨਿਆ ਮਨਿ ਕੀਤਾ ਭਾਉ॥
ਅੰਤਰਗਤਿ ਤੀਰਥਿ ਮਲਿ ਨਾਉ॥
ਸਭਿ ਗੁਣ ਤੇਰੇ ਮੈ ਨਾਹੀ ਕੋਇ॥
ਵਿਣੁ ਗੁਣ ਕੀਤੇ ਭਗਤਿ ਨ ਹੋਇ॥
ਸੁਅਸਤਿ ਆਥਿ ਬਾਣੀ ਬਰਮਾਉ॥
ਸਤਿ ਸੁਹਾਣੁ ਸਦਾ ਮਨਿ ਚਾਉ॥

stanza 21

In this stanza, Guru Nanak again asserts that the only way to attain realization is through contact with *Naam*. All conventional good deeds like pilgrimage, alms-giving, and acts of mercy, etc., asserts Guru Nanak, do not go a long way to attain any virtue of permanent value. The only source of all the permanent virtues is God the Almighty Himself, and, therefore, they can be acquired solely by contacting *Naam,* which flows from Him.

Pilgrimages, austerities, acts of mercy and giving of alms, such acts can earn us only transient honor. But one who listens to Naam, believes in Naam and cherishes love for Him in his heart washes away the sins of his soul at the fountain within us.

All virtues are Thine, none are mine, and without possessing virtue no worship is possible (i.e., I cannot possibly worship Thee without borrowing Thy virtues). Thou art Thyself Maya, the Word, the Brahma. Thou art Thyself Truth and Beauty enchantingly sweet. My soul yearns after Thee, O Lord. I hail Thee.

(continued on next page)

ਕਵਣੁ ਸੁ ਵੇਲਾ ਵਖਤੁ ਕਵਣੁ ਕਵਣ ਥਿਤਿ ਕਵਣੁ ਵਾਰੁ॥

ਕਵਣਿ ਸਿ ਰੁਤੀ ਮਾਹੁ ਕਵਣੁ ਜਿਤੁ ਹੋਆ ਆਕਾਰੁ॥

ਵੇਲ ਨ ਪਾਈਆ ਪੰਡਤੀ ਜਿ ਹੋਵੈ ਲੇਖੁ ਪੁਰਾਣੁ॥

ਵਖਤੁ ਨ ਪਾਇਓ ਕਾਦੀਆ ਜਿ ਲਿਖਨਿ ਲੇਖੁ ਕੁਰਾਣੁ॥

ਥਿਤਿ ਵਾਰੁ ਨਾ ਜੋਗੀ ਜਾਣੈ ਰੁਤਿ ਮਾਹੁ ਨਾ ਕੋਈ॥

ਜਾ ਕਰਤਾ ਸਿਰਠੀ ਕਉ ਸਾਜੇ ਆਪੇ ਜਾਣੈ ਸੋਈ॥

ਕਿਵ ਕਰਿ ਆਖਾ ਕਿਵ ਸਾਲਾਹੀ ਕਿਉ ਵਰਨੀ ਕਿਵ ਜਾਣਾ॥

ਨਾਨਕ ਆਖਣਿ ਸਭੁ ਕੋ ਆਖੈ ਇਕਦੂ ਇਕੁ ਸਿਆਣਾ॥

ਵਡਾ ਸਾਹਿਬੁ ਵਡੀ ਨਾਈ ਕੀਤਾ ਜਾ ਕਾ ਹੋਵੈ॥

ਨਾਨਕ ਜੇ ਕੋ ਆਪੌ ਜਾਣੈ ਅਗੈ ਗਇਆ ਨ ਸੋਹੈ॥ ੨੧॥

What was the time, the day of the week, the season and the month of the year when this world came into being? Pundits are not aware of this time, otherwise it would have been mentioned in the Holy Puranas, nor are the Qazis aware of it, otherwise they would have mentioned it in the Holy Quran, nor does the Jogi know about the time, the day the week, the season or the month of the year. This is known only to the Creator Himself.

How shall I address Thee, praise Thee, describe Thee, and know Thee? O Nanak, everybody claiming himself wiser than the others speaks of Thee.

O Nanak, if we are to go by our own intellect, we can simply say that great is the Lord and great are His qualities. Everything proceeds from His ordain. To say anything beyond this does not behoove us.

ਪਾਤਾਲਾ ਪਾਤਾਲ ਲਖ ਆਗਾਸਾ ਆਗਾਸ॥

ਓੜਕ ਓੜਕ ਭਾਲਿ ਥਕੇ ਵੇਦ ਕਹਨਿ ਇਕ ਵਾਤ॥

ਸਹਸ ਅਠਾਰਹ ਕਹਨਿ ਕਤੇਬਾ ਅਸੁਲੂ ਇਕੁ
ਧਾਤੁ॥

ਲੇਖਾ ਹੋਇ ਤ ਲਿਖੀਐ ਲੇਖੈ ਹੋਇ ਵਿਣਾਸੁ॥

ਨਾਨਕ ਵਡਾ ਆਖੀਐ ਆਪੇ ਜਾਣੈ ਆਪੁ॥ ੨੨॥

stanza 22

IN THIS STANZA, GURU NANAK TALKS OF THE INFINITENESS of this world, which eludes all attempts to comprehend it fully. Guru Nanak concludes that only God the Almighty Himself knows it fully.

There are worlds beyond this world, below as well as above it. All attempts to know the ends of them have to be given up in the end. The Vedas, thousands of intellectuals, the eighteen Puranas, and the other holy books all say only one thing: that the count of the worlds is beyond the count itself. O Nanak, God the Almighty Himself only knows about it.

Figure 13: Identified handwriting of Guru Nanak from the Guru Harsahai Pothi. Early 16th century.

Figure 12 (left): A rare early 19th century mural painting from Gurdwara Baba Atal depicting Guru Nanak. Mid to late 19th century.

ਸਾਲਾਹੀ ਸਾਲਾਹਿ ਏਤੀ ਸੁਰਤਿ ਨ ਪਾਈਆ॥

ਨਦੀਆ ਅਤੈ ਵਾਹ ਪਵਹਿ ਸਮੁੰਦਿ ਨ ਜਾਣੀਅਹਿ॥

ਸਮੁੰਦ ਸਾਹ ਸੁਲਤਾਨ ਗਿਰਹਾ ਸੇਤੀ ਮਾਲੁ ਧਨੁ॥

ਕੀੜੀ ਤੁਲਿ ਨ ਹੋਵਨੀ ਜੇ ਤਿਸੁ ਮਨਹੁ ਨ
ਵੀਸਰਹਿ॥ ੨੩॥

stanza 23

In this stanza, Guru Nanak stresses the infiniteness of the power of God the Almighty known only to Himself and emphasizes that no earthly possessions can equal the ever-lasting wealth of nursing love for the Lord.

The admirers of God the Almighty admire Him, and be one with Him, but still cannot know the extent of His greatness, just as rivers and rivulets fall into the sea, but know not its extent. The king with empire as vast as the oceans and possessing mountains of wealth is no match for an ant who does not forget the Lord.

ਅੰਤੁ ਨ ਸਿਫਤੀ ਕਹਣਿ ਨ ਅੰਤੁ ॥
ਅੰਤੁ ਨ ਕਰਣੈ ਦੇਣਿ ਨ ਅੰਤੁ ॥
ਅੰਤੁ ਨ ਵੇਖਣਿ ਸੁਣਣਿ ਨ ਅੰਤੁ ॥
ਅੰਤੁ ਨ ਜਾਪੈ ਕਿਆ ਮਨਿ ਮੰਤੁ ॥
ਅੰਤੁ ਨ ਜਾਪੈ ਕੀਤਾ ਆਕਾਰੁ ॥
ਅੰਤੁ ਨ ਜਾਪੈ ਪਾਰਾਵਾਰੁ ॥
ਅੰਤ ਕਾਰਣਿ ਕੇਤੇ ਬਿਲਲਾਹਿ ॥
ਤਾ ਕੇ ਅੰਤ ਨ ਪਾਏ ਜਾਹਿ ॥
ਏਹੁ ਅੰਤੁ ਨ ਜਾਣੈ ਕੋਇ ॥
ਬਹੁਤਾ ਕਹੀਐ ਬਹੁਤਾ ਹੋਇ ॥
ਵਡਾ ਸਾਹਿਬੁ ਊਚਾ ਥਾਉ ॥
ਊਚੇ ਉਪਰਿ ਊਚਾ ਨਾਉ ॥
ਏਵਡੁ ਊਚਾ ਹੋਵੈ ਕੋਇ ॥
ਤਿਸੁ ਊਚੇ ਕਉ ਜਾਣੈ ਸੋਇ ॥
ਜੇਵਡੁ ਆਪਿ ਜਾਣੈ ਆਪਿ ਆਪਿ ॥
ਨਾਨਕ ਨਦਰੀ ਕਰਮੀ ਦਾਤਿ ॥ ੨੪ ॥

stanza 24

Guru Nanak continues to describe the infiniteness of God the Almighty in this stanza.

There is no end to His qualities nor of their description. There is no end to His doings nor of His givings. There is no end to the sights and sounds, nor of His design. There is no end to the creation nor of its infinities. Many long to know the end, but His end knows no bounds. None know the end. The more it is described, the more it grows. Great is the Lord, and high is His abode, and still higher His qualities. Nobody can know His greatness without growing so great in stature. How great is He, He Himself knows. O Nanak, whatever we receive, receive through His kindness and grace.

ਬਹੁਤਾ ਕਰਮੁ ਲਿਖਿਆ ਨਾ ਜਾਇ॥

ਵਡਾ ਦਾਤਾ ਤਿਲੁ ਨ ਤਮਾਇ॥

ਕੇਤੇ ਮੰਗਹਿ ਜੋਧ ਅਪਾਰ॥

ਕੇਤਿਆ ਗਣਤ ਨਹੀ ਵੀਚਾਰੁ॥

ਕੇਤੇ ਖਪਿ ਤੁਟਹਿ ਵੇਕਾਰ॥

ਕੇਤੇ ਲੈ ਲੈ ਮੁਕਰੁ ਪਾਹਿ॥

ਕੇਤੇ ਮੂਰਖ ਖਾਹੀ ਖਾਹਿ॥

ਕੇਤਿਆ ਦੂਖ ਭੂਖ ਸਦ ਮਾਰ॥

ਏਹਿ ਭਿ ਦਾਤਿ ਤੇਰੀ ਦਾਤਾਰ॥

ਬੰਦਿ ਖਲਾਸੀ ਭਾਣੈ ਹੋਇ॥

ਹੋਰੁ ਆਖਿ ਨ ਸਕੈ ਕੋਇ॥

ਜੇ ਕੋ ਖਾਇਕੁ ਆਖਣਿ ਪਾਇ॥

ਓਹੁ ਜਾਣੈ ਜੇਤੀਆ ਮੁਹਿ ਖਾਇ॥

ਆਪੇ ਜਾਣੈ ਆਪੇ ਦੇਇ॥

ਆਖਹਿ ਸਿ ਭਿ ਕੇਈ ਕੇਇ॥

ਜਿਸਨੋ ਬਖਸੇ ਸਿਫਤਿ ਸਾਲਾਹ॥

ਨਾਨਕ ਪਾਤਿਸਾਹੀ ਪਾਤਿਸਾਹੁ॥ ੨੫॥

स्तन्ज़ा 25

His benevolence is beyond any description, yet the great Benefactor covets nothing at all in return. Countless warriors and also innumerable others beg of Him for His blessings. There are many who receive His blessings, but spend them in vices. There are many others who receive His blessings without feeling obliged. There are many gluttons who are fed on His bounties. There are also many who are afflicted even with pain and sufferings. This too is Thy benefaction, O Great Benefactor. The salvation from bondage is possible only by accepting His Will. Nobody can think of any other way out. If any fool tries to speak of any other way out, he alone knows how many blows he receives in the face. God alone knows our needs, and He alone fulfills them, but this fact is acknowledged by some (blessed) few. He who praises God the Almighty, being blessed with such a frame of mind, is, O Nanak, king of kings.

ਅਮੁਲ ਗੁਣ ਅਮੁਲ ਵਾਪਾਰ॥

ਅਮੁਲ ਵਾਪਾਰੀਏ ਅਮੁਲ ਭੰਡਾਰ॥

ਅਮੁਲ ਆਵਹਿ ਅਮੁਲ ਲੈ ਜਾਹਿ॥

ਅਮੁਲ ਭਾਇ ਅਮੁਲਾ ਸਮਾਹਿ॥

ਅਮੁਲੁ ਧਰਮੁ ਅਮੁਲੁ ਦੀਬਾਣੁ॥

ਅਮੁਲੁ ਤੁਲੁ ਅਮੁਲੁ ਪਰਵਾਣੁ॥

ਅਮੁਲੁ ਬਖਸੀਸ ਅਮੁਲੁ ਨੀਸਾਣੁ॥

ਅਮੁਲੁ ਕਰਮੁ ਅਮੁਲੁ ਫੁਰਮਾਣੁ॥

ਅਮੁਲੋ ਅਮੁਲੁ ਆਖਿਆ ਨ ਜਾਇ॥

ਆਖਿ ਆਖਿ ਰਹੇ ਲਿਵ ਲਾਇ॥

ﬆanza 26

In this stanza, again, the infiniteness of God the Almighty is proclaimed.

Invaluable are His qualities and invaluable the trade in them. Invaluable are the trades and the stock in trade. Priceless are the customers and priceless their purchase. With invaluable love for God the Almighty, they are absorbed in the Almighty Himself.

Priceless are His laws and priceless the administration. Priceless are His weights and priceless the measures. Priceless are His bounties and priceless the mark of His acceptance. Priceless are His mercies and priceless His commands.

Pricelessness of Priceless is beyond description. Those who try to describe it are lost in the end in Him.

(continued on next page)

ਆਖਹਿ ਵੇਦ ਪਾਠ ਪੁਰਾਣ॥
ਆਖਹਿ ਪੜੇ ਕਰਹਿ ਵਖਿਆਣ॥
ਆਖਹਿ ਬਰਮੇ ਆਖਹਿ ਇੰਦ॥
ਆਖਹਿ ਗੋਪੀ ਤੈ ਗੋਵਿੰਦ॥
ਆਖਹਿ ਈਸਰ ਆਖਹਿ ਸਿਧ॥
ਆਖਹਿ ਕੇਤੇ ਕੀਤੇ ਬੁਧ॥
ਆਖਹਿ ਦਾਨਵ ਆਖਹਿ ਦੇਵ॥
ਆਖਹਿ ਸੁਰਿ ਨਰ ਮੁਨਿ ਜਨ ਸੇਵ॥
ਕੇਤੇ ਆਖਹਿ ਆਖਣਿ ਪਾਹਿ॥
ਕੇਤੇ ਕਹਿ ਕਹਿ ਉਠਿ ਉਠਿ ਜਾਹਿ॥
ਏਤੇ ਕੀਤੇ ਹੋਰਿ ਕਰੇਹਿ॥
ਤਾ ਆਖਿ ਨ ਸਕਹਿ ਕੇਈ ਕੇਇ॥
ਜੇਵਡੁ ਭਾਵੈ ਤੇਵਡੁ ਹੋਇ॥
ਨਾਨਕ ਜਾਣੈ ਸਾਚਾ ਸੋਇ॥
ਜੇ ਕੋ ਆਖੈ ਬੋਲੁ ਵਿਗਾੜੁ॥
ਤਾ ਲਿਖੀਐ ਸਿਰਿ ਗਾਵਾਰਾ ਗਾਵਾਰੁ॥ ੨੬॥

The texts of Vedas and Puranas describe him. The learned describe Him, and deliver discourses about Him. Lord Brahma and Lord Indra, Lord Krishna and his gopis, all describe Him. Lord Shiva and his sidhas describe him. The demons and the gods, the sages and seers all describe Him. Many depart describing Him. His complete description still remains, and shall ever remain impossible.

He can grow as large as He pleases, and only Himself knows His complete self. Whosoever claims to know Him is the fool of fools.

Figure 14: The Gurdwara Janam Asthan in Nankana Sahib, Pakistan—the site where Nanak is believed to have been born.

Figure 15 (right): A Minaret of Gurdwara Janam Asthan.

ਸੋ ਦਰੁ ਕੇਹਾ ਸੋ ਘਰੁ ਕੇਹਾ ਜਿਤੁ ਬਹਿ ਸਰਬ ਸਮਾਲੇ॥

ਵਾਜੇ ਨਾਦ ਅਨੇਕ ਅਸੰਖਾ ਕੇਤੇ ਵਾਵਣਹਾਰੇ॥

ਕੇਤੇ ਰਾਗ ਪਰੀ ਸਿਉ ਕਹੀਅਨਿ ਕੇਤੇ ਗਾਵਣਹਾ-ਰੇ॥

ਗਾਵਹਿ ਤੁਹਨੋ ਪਉਣੁ ਪਾਣੀ ਬੈਸੰਤਰੁ ਗਾਵੈ ਰਾਜਾ-ਧਰਮੁ ਦੁਆਰੇ॥

ਗਾਵਹਿ ਚਿਤੁ ਗੁਪਤੁ ਲਿਖਿ ਜਾਣਹਿ ਲਿਖਿ ਲਿਖਿ ਧਰਮੁ ਵੀਚਾਰੇ॥

॒ङ्tanza 27

Here Guru Nanak talks of Divine Music heard in the higher regions, being sung in praise of God the Almighty. Guru Nanak concludes by repeating his advice to resign ourselves to the Will of God the Almighty.

What sort of gate and mansion is that where Thou sittest, and controleth the whole world? (I hear) several and innumerable melodious sounds made by several musicians. (I hear) songs being sung by many singers.

The air, water and fire all sing in Thy praise. Dharam raja, the king of death, also sings Thy praise standing at your door. Chit-gupts, the recording angels whose records are considered by Dharam raja in weighing men's deeds, also sing in Thy praise.

(continued on next page)

ਗਾਵਹਿ ਈਸਰੁ ਬਰਮਾ ਦੇਵੀ ਸੋਹਨਿ ਸਦਾ ਸਵਾਰੇ॥

ਗਾਵਹਿ ਇੰਦ ਇਦਾਸਣਿ ਬੈਠੇ ਦੇਵਤਿਆ ਦਰਿ ਨਾਲੇ॥

ਗਾਵਹਿ ਸਿਧ ਸਮਾਧੀ ਅੰਦਰਿ ਗਾਵਨਿ ਸਾਧ ਵਿਚਾਰੇ॥

ਗਾਵਨਿ ਜਤੀ ਸਤੀ ਸੰਤੋਖੀ ਗਾਵਹਿ ਵੀਰ ਕਰਾਰੇ॥

ਗਾਵਨਿ ਪੰਡਿਤ ਪੜਨਿ ਰਖੀਸਰ ਜੁਗੁ ਜੁਗੁ ਵੇਦਾ ਨਾਲੇ॥

ਗਾਵਹਿ ਮੋਹਣੀਆ ਮਨੁ ਮੋਹਨਿ ਸੁਰਗਾ ਮਛ ਪਇਆਲੇ॥

ਗਾਵਨਿ ਰਤਨ ਉਪਾਏ ਤੇਰੇ ਅਠਸਠਿ ਤੀਰਥ ਨਾਲੇ॥

The god Shiva, the god Brahma, and goddesses and also those graced by Thee are adoring Thy durbar. The god Indra sitting on his throne along with the angels is singing Thy praise.

The siddhas in their meditation and sadhus in the contemplation, and men pure in heart and endowed with patience and perseverance, and also those who are mighty warriors, all sing Thy praise.

The learned pundits of Vedas and rishis (seers) all sing Thee through ages. The bewitching maidens who inhabit the earth, the upper and lower regions, sing Thy praise.

The gems created by Thee, the sixty-eight places of pilgrimage, the warriors of mighty strength, the four sources of creation, the regions of earth and spheres of the universe, created and supported by Thee, all sing Thee, O Lord.

(continued on next page)

ਗਾਵਹਿ ਜੋਧ ਮਹਾਬਲ ਸੂਰਾ ਗਾਵਹਿ ਖਾਣੀ ਚਾਰੇ॥

ਗਾਵਹਿ ਖੰਡ ਮੰਡਲ ਵਰਭੰਡਾ ਕਰਿ ਕਰਿ ਰਖੇ ਧਾਰੇ॥

ਸੇਈ ਤੁਧੁਨੋ ਗਾਵਹਿ ਜੋ ਤੁਧੁ ਭਾਵਨਿ ਰਤੇ ਤੇਰੇ ਭਗਤ ਰਸਾਲੇ॥

ਹੋਰਿ ਕੇਤੇ ਗਾਵਨਿ ਸੇ ਮੈ ਚਿਤਿ ਨ ਆਵਨਿ ਨਾਨਕੁ ਕਿਆ ਵੀਚਾਰੇ॥

ਸੋਈ ਸੋਈ ਸਦਾ ਸਚੁ ਸਾਹਿਬੁ ਸਾਚਾ ਸਾਚੀ ਨਾਈ॥

ਹੈ ਭੀ ਹੋਸੀ ਜਾਇ ਨ ਜਾਸੀ ਰਚਨਾ ਜਿਨਿ ਰਚਾਈ॥

ਰੰਗੀ ਰੰਗੀ ਭਾਤੀ ਕਰਿ ਕਰਿ ਜਿਨਸੀ ਮਾਇਆ ਜਿਨਿ ਉਪਾਈ॥

ਕਰਿ ਕਰਿ ਵੇਖੈ ਕੀਤਾ ਆਪਣਾ ਜਿਵ ਤਿਸ ਦੀ ਵਡਿਆਈ॥

ਜੋ ਤਿਸੁ ਭਾਵੈ ਸੋਈ ਕਰਸੀ ਹੁਕਮੁ ਨ ਕਰਣਾ ਜਾਈ॥

ਸੋ ਪਾਤਿਸਾਹੁ ਸਾਹਾ ਪਾਤਿਸਾਹਿਬੁ ਨਾਨਕ ਰਹਣੁ ਰਜਾਈ॥ ੨੧॥

Those whom you like and who are steeped in Thy love sing Thee. Many others too acclaim Thee, whom I cannot recollect. So, what I can I say of them.

The Almighty who has created this creation is the Only One who will endure forever, and also will endure forever His greatness. He is present and shall continue to be present. The Lord who has created things of different hues and species beholds His handiwork, as it behooves Him. The Lord will do as He wills, as no order to Him can issue. He is King of kings; O Nanak, conduct thyself according to His Will.

ਮੁੰਦਾ ਸੰਤੋਖੁ ਸਰਮੁ ਪਤੁ ਝੋਲੀ ਧਿਆਨ ਕੀ ਕਰਹਿ ਬਿਭੂਤਿ॥

ਖਿੰਥਾ ਕਾਲੁ ਕੁਆਰੀ ਕਾਇਆ ਜੁਗਤਿ ਡੰਡਾ ਪਰਤੀਤਿ॥

ਆਈ ਪੰਥੀ ਸਗਲ ਜਮਾਤੀ ਮਨਿ ਜੀਤੈ ਜਗੁ ਜੀਤੁ॥

ਆਦੇਸੁ ਤਿਸੈ ਆਦੇਸੁ॥

ਆਦਿ ਅਨੀਲੁ ਅਨਾਦਿ ਅਨਾਹਤਿ ਜੁਗੁ ਜੁਗੁ ਏਕੋ ਵੇਸੁ॥ ੨੮॥

stanza 28

HERE GURU NANAK TALKS OF THE OUTWARDLY FORM AD-
opted by *yogis* (hermits) of his days. The highest sect among
the *yogis* considered those days was that of '*Aee Panthees*.'
Even they cared too much for their outwardly form and little for their inwardly qualities. Guru Nanak, with the help of
a beautiful metaphor, suggests the real qualities which go to
make *yogis* and highest sect among them.

> O, yogi, let contentment be your ear-rings, efforts
> be your begging bowl, meditation be your ash to
> be smeared on your body, the fear of death be your
> mat to rest, chastity be your way of life, and faith
> be your staff to lean on. The highest sect of yogis
> is the one that believes in universal brotherhood,
> the greatest victory, the victory over self. Let us
> bow to Him alone—The Primal, Pure, Eternal,
> and Immutable.

ਭੁਗਤਿ ਗਿਆਨੁ ਦਇਆ ਭੰਡਾਰਣਿ ਘਟਿ ਘਟਿ ਵਾਜਹਿ ਨਾਦ॥

ਆਪਿ ਨਾਥੁ ਨਾਥੀ ਸਭ ਜਾ ਕੀ ਰਿਧਿ ਸਿਧਿ ਅਵਰਾ ਸਾਦ॥

ਸੰਜੋਗੁ ਵਿਜੋਗੁ ਦੁਇ ਕਾਰ ਚਲਾਵਹਿ ਲੇਖੇ ਆਵਹਿ ਭਾਗ॥

ਆਦੇਸੁ ਤਿਸੈ ਆਦੇਸੁ॥

ਆਦਿ ਅਨੀਲੁ ਅਨਾਦਿ ਅਨਾਹਤਿ ਜੁਗੁ ਜੁਗੁ ਏਕੋ ਵੇਸੁ॥ ੨੯॥

stanza 29

THE THEME OF STANZA 28 CONTINUES IN THE PRESENT stanza.

(O yogi,) Let the knowledge of Divine be your food, mercy be your steward, and the music of spheres the conch shell blown by you. The Lord alone controls the whole universe. Aiming at attainment of supernatural powers is drifting away from Him. By the two tools of union and separation, He is managing the affairs of this universe, and everyone receives the share according to His ordain. Let us bow to Him alone—The Primal, Pure, Eternal, and Immutable.

ਏਕਾ ਮਾਈ ਜੁਗਤਿ ਵਿਆਈ ਤਿਨਿ ਚੇਲੇ ਪਰਵਾਣੁ॥

ਇਕੁ ਸੰਸਾਰੀ ਇਕੁ ਭੰਡਾਰੀ ਇਕੁ ਲਾਏ ਦੀ ਬਾਣੁ॥

ਜਿਵ ਤਿਸੁ ਭਾਵੈ ਤਿਵੈ ਚਲਾਵੈ ਜਿਵ ਹੋਵੈ ਫੁਰਮਾਣੁ॥

ਓਹੁ ਵੇਖੈ ਓਨਾ ਨਦਰਿ ਨ ਆਵੈ ਬਹੁਤਾ ਏਹੁ ਵਿਡਾਣੁ॥

ਆਦੇਸੁ ਤਿਸੈ ਆਦੇਸੁ॥

ਆਦਿ ਅਨੀਲੁ ਅਨਾਦਿ ਅਨਾਹਤਿ ਜੁਗੁ ਜੁਗੁ ਏਕੋ ਵੇਸੁ॥ ੩੦॥

stanza 30

Here Guru Nanak refers to the supremacy of Will of God the Almighty and states that the three gods running the affairs of the world are working directly under His command.

Maya (the mythical goddess) in wedlock Divine gave birth to three gods (Brahma, Vishnu, and Shiva) the creator, sustainer and destroyer. They, however, do their respective duties as is willed and ordered by God the Almighty. The great wonder it is that while He beholds them, He Himself remains unseen by them. O, bow to Him alone—The Primal, Pure, Eternal, Immortal, and Immutable through all ages.

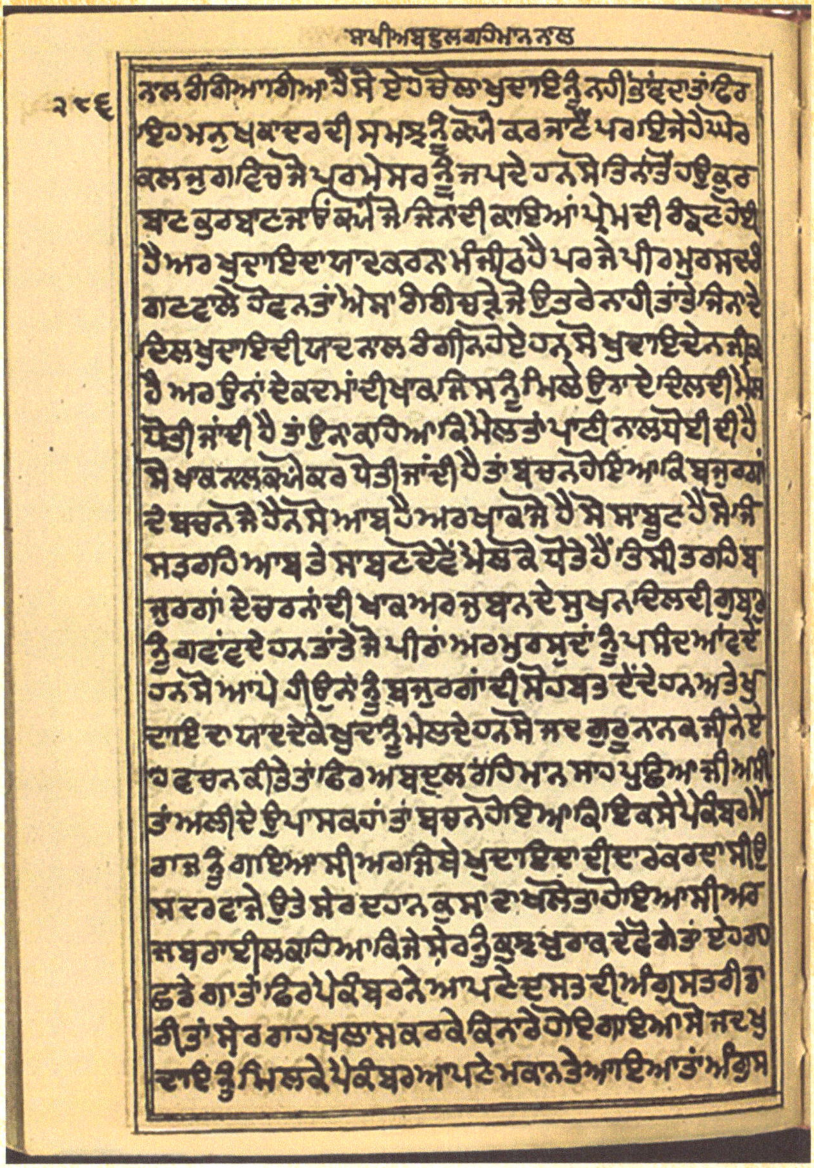

Figure 17: Bhai Mani Singh's Janamsakhi (biographical sources on Guru Nanak's life) was originally written in 1712. This reproduction is likely circa 19th century.

Figure 16 (left): Birth of Guru Nanak, painting from an 1830's Janamsakhi.

ਆਸਣੁ ਲੋਇ ਲੋਇ ਭੰਡਾਰ॥

ਜੋ ਕਿਛੁ ਪਾਇਆ ਸੁ ਏਕਾ ਵਾਰ॥

ਕਰਿ ਕਰਿ ਵੇਖੈ ਸਿਰਜਣਹਾਰੁ॥

ਨਾਨਕ ਸਚੇ ਕੀ ਸਾਚੀ ਕਾਰ॥

ਆਦੇਸੁ ਤਿਸੈ ਆਦੇਸੁ॥

ਆਦਿ ਅਨੀਲੁ ਅਨਾਦਿ ਅਨਾਹਤਿ ਜੁਗੁ ਜੁਗੁ ਏਕੋ ਵੇਸੁ॥ ੩੧॥

stanza 31

Here Guru Nanak talks of the omnipresence of God the Almighty and the adequacy of His arrangement.

God the Almighty dwells in all the regions and has His never-exhausting stores there. Having been stocked once, they require no replenishment. He creates His creation, and watches over it. O Nanak, true are the words of Truthful. O, bow to Him alone—The Primal, Pure, Eternal, Immortal, and Immutable through all ages.

ਇਕਦੂ ਜੀਭੌ ਲਖ ਹੋਹਿ ਲਖ ਹੋਵਹਿ ਲਖ ਵੀਸ॥
ਲਖੁ ਲਖੁ ਗੇੜਾ ਆਖੀਅਹਿ ਏਕੁ ਨਾਮੁ ਜਗਦੀਸ॥
ਏਤੁ ਰਾਹਿ ਪਤਿ ਪਵੜੀਆ ਚੜੀਐ ਹੋਇ ਇਕੀਸ॥
ਸੁਣਿ ਗਲਾ ਆਕਾਸ ਕੀ ਕੀਟਾ ਆਈ ਰੀਸ॥
ਨਾਨਕ ਨਦਰੀ ਪਾਈਐ ਕੂੜੀ ਕੂੜੈ ਠੀਸ॥ ੩੨॥

stanza 32

Here Guru Nanak advises us to nurse intense love for Him, as freedom from bondage is possible only through His Grace.

If I were to have a hundred thousand tongues, and each of them were to multiply twenty times, I would utter name of the Almighty, a hundreds of thousands times with each of the tongues. This way lies the steps leading to Him, ascending which one becomes one with Him. Hearing the talk concerning Heaven, even the petty insects aspire to reach there. [Guru Nanak compares himself to a petty insect.] But be it borne clearly in mind that contact to Him can be had only through His Grace. That He can be contacted otherwise also is mere lie.

ਆਖਣਿ ਜੋਰੁ ਚੁਪੈ ਨਹ ਜੋਰੁ॥

ਜੋਰੁ ਨ ਮੰਗਣਿ ਦੇਣਿ ਨ ਜੋਰੁ॥

ਜੋਰੁ ਨ ਜੀਵਣਿ ਮਰਣਿ ਨਹ ਜੋਰੁ॥

ਜੋਰੁ ਨ ਰਾਜਿ ਮਾਲਿ ਮਨਿ ਸੋਰੁ॥

ਜੋਰੁ ਨ ਸੁਰਤੀ ਗਿਆਨਿ ਵੀਚਾਰਿ॥

ਜੋਰੁ ਨ ਜੁਗਤੀ ਛੁਟੈ ਸੰਸਾਰੁ॥

ਜਿਸੁ ਹਥਿ ਜੋਰੁ ਕਰਿ ਵੇਖੈ ਸੋਇ॥

ਨਾਨਕ ਉਤਮੁ ਨੀਚੁ ਨ ਕੋਇ॥ ੩੩॥

stanza 33

Here Guru Nanak asserts an utter helplessness to achieve anything without His Will.

We have no power speaking or remaining silent. We have no power over asking or granting any favor. We have no power to acquire wealth or status for which our mind constantly remains engaged.

We have no power over attaining spiritual upliftment or achieving knowledge divine. We have no power to attain salvation leaving this world for good. If anyone is having any doubt about this truth, let him try out for himself. O Nanak, there is none low or high, but by His Will.

ਰਾਤੀ ਰੁਤੀ ਥਿਤੀ ਵਾਰ॥

ਪਵਣ ਪਾਣੀ ਅਗਨੀ ਪਾਤਾਲ॥

ਤਿਸੁ ਵਿਚਿ ਧਰਤੀ ਥਾਪਿ ਰਖੀ ਧਰਮਸਾਲ॥

ਤਿਸੁ ਵਿਚਿ ਜੀਅ ਜੁਗਤਿ ਕੇ ਰੰਗ॥

ਤਿਨ ਕੇ ਨਾਮ ਅਨੇਕ ਅਨੰਤ॥

ਕਰਮੀ ਕਰਮੀ ਹੋਇ ਵੀਚਾਰੁ॥

ਸਚਾ ਆਪਿ ਸਚਾ ਦਰਬਾਰੁ॥

ਤਿਥੈ ਸੋਹਨਿ ਪੰਚ ਪਰਵਾਣੁ॥

ਨਦਰੀ ਕਰਮਿ ਪਵੈ ਨੀਸਾਣੁ॥

ਕਚ ਪਕਾਈ ਓਥੈ ਪਾਇ॥

ਨਾਨਕ ਗਇਆ ਜਾਪੈ ਜਾਇ॥ ੩੪॥

Stanza 34

In Stanzas 34-37, Guru Nanak surveys one after another the various spiritual regions, viz. *Dharm-Khand, Gian-Khand, Sarm-Khand, Karm-Khand* and *Sach-Khand,* through which soul must travel to reach God the Almighty.

The Almighty created the day and night, the seasons, the periods of time. He created the air, the water, the fire, and lower regions, and among all these He created this world—the field of action. In this world He created creatures of different hues with infinite names.

True is God and True is His court, and everyone is judged according to His deeds. Those honored by Him (the Chiefs) adorn His court. This distinction is conferred only through His Grace. The imperfect attain perfection there. O Nanak, this is revealed only on reaching there.

ਧਰਮ ਖੰਡ ਕਾ ਏਹੋ ਧਰਮੁ॥

ਗਿਆਨ ਖੰਡ ਕਾ ਆਖਹੁ ਕਰਮੁ॥

ਪਵਣ ਪਾਣੀ ਵੈਸੰਤਰ ਕੇ ਤੇ ਕਾਨ ਮਹੇਸ॥

ਕੇਤੇ ਬਰਮੇ ਘਾੜਤਿ ਘੜੀਅਹਿ ਰੂਪ ਰੰਗ ਕੇ ਵੇਸ॥

ਕੇਤੀਆ ਕਰਮਭੂਮੀ ਮੇਰ ਕੇਤੇ ਕੇਤੇ ਧੁ ਉਪਦੇਸ॥

ਕੇਤੇ ਇੰਦ ਚੰਦ ਸੂਰ ਕੇਤੇ ਕੇਤੇ ਮੰਡਲ ਦੇਸ॥

ਕੇਤੇ ਸਿਧ ਬੁਧ ਨਾਥ ਕੇਤੇ ਕੇਤੇ ਦੇਵੀ ਵੇਸ॥

ਕੇਤੇ ਦੇਵ ਦਾਨਵ ਮੁਨਿ ਕੇਤੇ ਕੇਤੇ ਰਤਨ ਸਮੁੰਦ॥

ਕੇਤੀਆ ਖਾਣੀ ਕੇਤੀਆ ਬਾਣੀ ਕੇਤੇ ਪਾਤ ਨਰਿੰਦ॥

ਕੇਤੀਆ ਸੁਰਤੀ ਸੇਵਕ ਕੇਤੇ ਨਾਨਕ ਅੰਤੁ ਨ ਅੰਤੁ॥
੩੫॥

stanza 35

After having described the realm of action, I now describe the realm of knowledge. Countless are its elements of water, air, fire. Countless are its Krishnas and Shivas—the gods that preserve and destroy. Countless are Brahmas fashioning creatures of different forms and colours.

Countless are fields of actions, countless the golden mountains and countless the Dhrus[4] meditating therein. Countless are the thunders and lightening, the suns and the moons. Countless are the demigods. Countless the bejeweled seas. Countless are the sources of creation, countless the languages and countless the type of kings. Countless are the harmonies and countless the devotees. O Nanak, countless and unending is the description of this realm.

---

[4] Saint Dhrus, well known for his meditation

103

ਗਿਆਨ ਖੰਡ ਮਹਿ ਗਿਆਨੁ ਪਰਚੰਡੁ॥

ਤਿਥੈ ਨਾਦ ਬਿਨੋਦ ਕੋਡ ਅਨੰਦੁ॥

ਸਰਮ ਖੰਡ ਕੀ ਬਾਣੀ ਰੂਪੁ॥

ਤਿਥੈ ਘਾੜਤਿ ਘੜੀਐ ਬਹੁਤੁ ਅਨੂਪੁ॥

ਤਾ ਕੀਆ ਗਲਾ ਕਥੀਆ ਨਾ ਜਾਹਿ॥

ਜੇ ਕੋ ਕਹੈ ਪਿਛੈ ਪਛੁਤਾਇ॥

ਤਿਥੈ ਘੜੀਐ ਸੁਰਤਿ ਮਤਿ ਮਨਿ ਬੁਧਿ॥

ਤਿਥੈ ਘੜੀਐ ਸੁਰਾ ਸਿਧਾ ਕੀ ਸੁਧਿ॥ ੩੬॥

stanza 36

Divine knowledge rules supreme in Gian-Khand—the realm of knowledge. Here divine music yields (limitless) joy and bliss. Beauty is characteristic of Sarm-Khand, the realm of Ecstasy. There are fashioned forms of supreme beauty. The description of that realm is beyond possibility. Whosoever attempts to do so has to repent afterwards. There are sharpened consciousness, understanding, mind and reasons. There is attained the insight of the gods and the sages.

ਕਰਮ ਖੰਡ ਕੀ ਬਾਣੀ ਜੋਰੁ॥
ਤਿਥੈ ਹੋਰੁ ਨ ਕੋਈ ਹੋਰੁ॥
ਤਿਥੈ ਜੋਧ ਮਹਾਬਲ ਸੂਰ॥
ਤਿਨ ਮਹਿ ਰਾਮੁ ਰਹਿਆ ਭਰਪੂਰ॥
ਤਿਥੈ ਸੀਤੋ ਸੀਤਾ ਮਹਿਮਾ ਮਾਹਿ॥
ਤਾ ਕੇ ਰੂਪ ਨ ਕਥਨੇ ਜਾਹਿ॥
ਨਾ ਓਹਿ ਮਰਹਿ ਨ ਠਾਗੇ ਜਾਹਿ॥
ਜਿਨ ਕੈ ਰਾਮੁ ਵਸੈ ਮਨ ਮਾਹਿ॥
ਤਿਥੈ ਭਗਤ ਵਸਹਿ ਕੇ ਲੋਅ॥
ਕਰਹਿ ਅਨੰਦੁ ਸਚਾ ਮਨਿ ਸੋਇ॥
ਸਚਖੰਡਿ ਵਸੈ ਨਿਰੰਕਾਰੁ॥
ਕਰਿ ਕਰਿ ਵੇਖੈ ਨਦਰਿ ਨਿਹਾਲ॥
ਤਿਥੈ ਖੰਡ ਮੰਡਲ ਵਰਭੰਡ॥
ਜੇ ਕੋ ਕਥੈ ਤ ਅੰਤ ਨ ਅੰਤ॥
ਤਿਥੈ ਲੋਅ ਲੋਅ ਆਕਾਰ॥
ਜਿਵ ਜਿਵ ਹੁਕਮੁ ਤਿਵੈ ਤਿਵ ਕਾਰ॥
ਵੇਖੈ ਵਿਗਸੈ ਕਰਿ ਵੀਚਾਰੁ॥
ਨਾਨਕ ਕਥਨਾ ਕਰੜਾ ਸਾਰੁ॥ ੩੭॥

stanza 37

Might characterizes Karm-Khand the Realm of Grace. Nothing other than Might pervades there. There dwell the bravest of men filled with the divine love. There dwell celestial maidens of beauty indescribable amid His glory. These can neither die nor be beguiled, as God Himself resides in their hearts. There the saints of all regions live in heavenly bliss, for God Himself resides in their hearts.

Sach-Khand, the Realm of Truth, is the seat of God the Almighty. Here He creates His creation, and lovingly watches it.

Here there are many regions, spheres and universes of endless description. Here are houses of different forms. Everything here moves according to His Ordain. From here He looks at His handiwork, rejoices and contemplates about it. O Nanak, it is a difficult task to give a complete description of this realm.

ਜਤੁ ਪਾਹਾਰਾ ਧੀਰਜੁ ਸੁਨਿਆਰੁ ॥
ਅਹਰਣਿ ਮਤਿ ਵੇਦੁ ਹਥੀਆਰੁ ॥
ਭਉ ਖਲਾ ਅਗਨਿ ਤਪ ਤਾਉ ॥
ਭਾਂਡਾ ਭਾਉ ਅੰਮ੍ਰਿਤੁ ਤਿਤੁ ਢਾਲਿ ॥
ਘੜੀਐ ਸਬਦੁ ਸਚੀ ਟਕਸਾਲ ॥
ਜਿਨ ਕਉ ਨਦਰਿ ਕਰਮੁ ਤਿਨ ਕਾਰ ॥
ਨਾਨਕ ਨਦਰੀ ਨਦਰਿ ਨਿਹਾਲ ॥ ੩੮ ॥

स्तंझ 38

Here Guru Nanak tells how to inculcate qualities of everlasting values. This he does by the help of a beautiful simile coined by him.

> To mint true coins of lasting value, let chastity be your furnace, patience the goldsmith, reason the anvil, true knowledge the hammer, fear of God the bellows to blow the fire. In the crucible of love pour divine liquid of nectar. Only those who are blessed by Him can take to this path. O Nanak, by His Grace they are filled with everlasting joy.

ਸਲੋਕੁ॥

ਪਵਣੁ ਗੁਰੂ ਪਾਣੀ ਪਿਤਾ ਮਾਤਾ ਧਰਤਿ ਮਹਤੁ॥

ਦਿਵਸੁ ਰਾਤਿ ਦੁਇ ਦਾਈ ਦਾਇਆ ਖੇਲੈ ਸਗਲ ਜਗਤੁ॥

ਚੰਗਿਆਈਆ ਬੁਰਿਆਈਆ ਵਾਚੈ ਧਰਮੁ ਹਦੂਰਿ॥

ਕਰਮੀ ਆਪੋ ਆਪਣੀ ਕੇ ਨੇੜੈ ਕੇ ਦੂਰਿ॥

ਜਿਨੀ ਨਾਮੁ ਧਿਆਇਆ ਗਏ ਮਸਕਤਿ ਘਾਲਿ॥

ਨਾਨਕ ਤੇ ਮੁਖ ਉਜਲੇ ਕੇਤੀ ਛੁਟੀ ਨਾਲਿ॥ ੧॥

the epilogue

Air is the Master, water the Father and earth our Mother. Day and night are the two nurses in whose lap play the whole world. The Almighty judges everyone according to the deeds, and it is according to our own deeds that we are cast away or kept near His seat. The toils of those who have worshipped God the Almighty shall be crowned with success. O Nanak, their faces shall be lit with glory. Not only they but many others along with them shall be set free.

Figure 18: Mr. Om Prakash Bakshi in his study at his residence, 1/121 Capper Road, Lalbagh, Lucknow, Uttar Pradesh, India, circa 1958. Evening studies for the family was part of the routine. (Bakshi Archives Image).

biographical note

BECAUSE OF THE SIGNIFICANCE THIS BOOK HAS TO BOTH me and my father, Mr. Om Prakash Bakshi, I found it appropriate to add a biographical note. Our family has history with teachers of these holy scriptures, such as Sant Kripal Singh who shared both a wall and a well with our father's ancestral home in the village of Sayyad Kasaran, now in Pakistan. Swami Sawan Singh ji, a teacher of Kripal Sign ji, frequented the home while the children of the home visited. My grandfather had built a 26 ft x 52 ft room with a wooden ceiling just for those spiritual meetings (Satsang). My uncle, Surinder Malhotra, recently told me stories of him going to the city of Beos with Swami Kripal Singh ji, while sitting in his lap!

The change to my father's last name permits another story to share. As it turned out my grandfather had great penmanship and could write equally well with both hands in Urdu, Panjabi, Farsi and English. In those days, before typewriters were available, his services were in great demand. One of his favorite pastimes was to write words inverted—urging the reader to look into a mirror to read what he had written. His reading and writing skills got attention of the British occupants in the area who began to call him by the nickname "Bakshi" or the learned one. So, his name became Bakshi Lal Chand Malhotra.

Figure 19: Mrs. Pushpa Bakshi (wife of the author and mother of the editor). She was a lecturer of Panjabi language in Guru Nanak Girls College in Lucknow, India. She had a MA in Punjabi and degree of Gyani (which authorized her to read the scripture Guru Granth Sahib), circa 1956. (Bakshi Archives Image).

After partition, my father decided to shorten everyone's name and made Bakshi (written as Bakhshi in Hindi and Urdu[5]) our last name. Such practice was not uncommon, as my father and millions of others moved east from Panjab, as India was separated into India and Pakistan. My mother's family also changed their last name from Oberoi to Bhagat. I believe they did so to better conform to their new surroundings.

For the sake of integration, my parents spoke to us in Hindi, which is not distinguished from Urdu in its spoken form. Urdu was the common language of Lucknow but not Panjabi— although there were many Panjabi speakers in Lucknow who had migrated there from Panjab. At the time, my father's knowledge of Panjabi came from what he wrote in Urdu script, as was the custom in those days. Panjabi in Urdu script, known as *Shahmukhi*, is a tradition that goes back centuries, hence the dictionary I used from Patiala gives words in both Gurmukhi and Urdu script. My maternal uncle even published a newspaper in Punjabi that was printed in Urdu script in New Delhi, until his death in the 1990s.

Vivek Bakshi (Editor)
November 11, 2025, Austin, Texas, USA

---

[5] From the *Glossary of Abu'l – Fazl The History of Akabar,* Vol I, Murti Classical Library of India, Harvard University Press, 2015 : Bakhshi – A word with complex history. originating with the Chinese as *bokshi* – Scholar, and adopted by Mongols as *bagshi,* for Buddhist teachers, under the Timurids in India it developed into a title for high military positions, something like a paymaster and chief of staff. In Anglo-India it was also became "buxee."

Figure 20: Mr. Om Prakash Bakshi and Mrs. Pushpa Bakshi, team behind the translation, circa 1956. (Bakshi Archives Image).

Figure 21: Editor Vivek Bakshi with his parents at the terrace of their residence, 1/121 Capper Road, Lalbagh, Lucknow, Uttar Pradesh, India. A large amount of family time was spent on this terrace, working, playing and also for studies, circa 1975. (Bakshi Archives Image).

Figure 22: Mr. Om Prakash Bakshi with his three elder brothers. Clockwise from top left: Baljeet Kumar Bakshi, Om Prakash Bakshi, Pran Nath Malhotra, and Faqir Chand Bakshi. All four led deeply spiritual lives. The family had a long-standing tradition of organizing and participating in Satsang under the guidance of the Radha Soami tradition of Swami Kirpal Singh. They carried forward a rich heritage that combined Hindu and Sikh spiritual practices, brought from their ancestral village of Syed Kasran (now in Pakistan). This tradition continues within the family to this day, including through their brother Surinder Malhotra (not pictured), circa late 1970s–early 1980s. (Bakshi Archives Image).

Figure 23: Mrs. Kartar Devi Kaur, a devout Sikh and grandmother of the editor, circa 1970s. She is shown holding a Gutka Sahib and her prayer beads, which she was rarely seen without. The Gutka Sahib is a collection of Sikh prayers and hymns, particularly the daily Nitnem prayers, drawn from the Guru Granth Sahib and Dasam Granth. It includes, among other prayers, Japuji Sahib. Affectionately known as Nani ji, she lived to the age of 92, spending her days in devoted prayer. (Bakshi Archives Image).

biography of om prakash bakshi (1932–1999)

ਸੋਚਿ ਸੋਚਿ ਨਾ ਹੋਵਈ ਜੇ ਸੋਚੀ ਲਖ ਵਾਰ ॥

Soci soc na hovai je socī lakh vār.
By mere thinking, one cannot comprehend the Truth, even by thinking hundreds of thousands of times.
  —Japuji Sahib, Stanza 1

ਸੁਣਿਐ ਦੂਖ ਪਾਪ ਕਾ ਨਾਸ ॥੫॥

Suṇi-ai dukh pāp kā nās.
By deep listening and understanding, pain and sin are erased.
  —Japuji Sahib, Stanza 8

early years and family roots

Om Prakash Bakshi was born on March 12, 1932, in Sayad Kasarn, a small village in British India, now part of Pakistan. The youngest of six children in a prosperous family of landowners, his childhood was one of warmth, learning, and quiet abundance. He often recalled riding on horseback after harvest to choose one of two piles of grain set aside by tenant farmers—a ritual that taught him fairness and humility.

The Bakshi home included a 24 ft × 36 ft hall built for spiritual gatherings and shared a wall and well with the home of

120

Sant Kirpal Singh, disciple of Swami Sawan Singh Ji Maharaj. This proximity to the saints of the Radha Soami tradition left a lasting spiritual impression that later shaped his approach to faith and the Japuji Sahib.

partition and resettlement

THE PARTITION OF INDIA IN 1947 CHANGED HIS LIFE FOR-ever. Separated from home and heritage, he fled on foot to New Delhi while his aged grandmother remained behind. In Delhi he completed his studies through special examinations organized for refugee students.

To support himself, he learned typing and earned a modest living by drafting letters for those seeking legal help—an early sign of both his empathy and his disciplined intellect.

education and professional life

OM PRAKASH LATER JOINED THE TELECOMMUNICATIONS Department of Uttar Pradesh. When the state capital moved to Lucknow, he relocated there and made the city his permanent home.

He earned his B.A. and M.A. in English Literature from Lucknow University, becoming the first in his family to hold a graduate degree—inspiring his wife to later pursue her M.A. in Punjabi. Fluent in Punjabi and Urdu, he mastered Hindi and English, often entertaining guests with heartfelt recitations from Shakespeare.

His command of language and the typewriter made him an indispensable friend and colleague. Though health concerns kept him from completing an LLB degree, his fascination with law and reasoning endured throughout his life.

a life of reflection and faith

BENEATH HIS CALM DEMEANOR LIVED A RESTLESS SEEKER. Om Prakash approached spirituality not through ritual but through understanding. He believed that faith must be examined, not merely inherited. His translation of the Japuji Sahib emerged from decades of study, reading, and reflection. Each verse, he felt, contained layers of meaning—moral, poetic, and metaphysical—accessible only through both intellect and reverence.

Evenings in his home were filled with quiet discussions on philosophy, law, and the mysteries of the spirit. For him, study was a form of prayer, and language a path to the divine.

family and daily devotion

AT HOME, OM PRAKASH WAS A MAN OF REMARKABLE SIMplicity. He shared in every household duty—unusual for his generation—to support his wife, who also worked full-time. He took pride in visiting the local market each morning for fresh vegetables and milk, and personally cooked the evening sabji for the family.

Even after his elder son's marriage, he continued his daily errands, offering quiet care that became the rhythm of family life. His steadiness, kindness, and humor made him the trusted counselor of friends and relatives alike.

legacy and remembrance

OM PRAKASH BAKSHI LIVED IN LUCKNOW FROM THE MID-1950s until his passing in 1999, at the age of 67. He was the first among his siblings to depart this world but remains ever-present through his words and example.

His translation of the Japuji Sahib is both a spiritual offering and a record of a life devoted to understanding—bridging intellect and faith, word and spirit.

He is remembered as a scholar, family man, and gentle teacher who believed that "understanding itself is prayer." His life continues to inspire those who seek truth with humility, compassion, and reasoned faith.

Vivek Bakshi (Editor)
November 11, 2025, Austin, Texas, USA

glossary[6]

Aee Panthees – Follower of a sect of yogis called *Aee*

Brahma Vishnu, Shiva – Holy trinity per Hindus, responsible for creation, sustaining and ending of the world

Gopi – Female devotees of Krishna, usually cow-herders

Moksha – Enlightenment

Naam – Same as Nada or divine sound

Nada – Creative power of God also called *Naam*, ordinarily meaning of word is sound

Natha – Master or God, also a sect of Hindu ascetics

Nirvana – Enlightenment

Pir – Muslim spiritual teacher

Puranas – Ancient Hindu scriptures

Qazis – Muslim priest

Sidha – Spiritual being with divine powers

---

[6] Added by Vivek Bakshi

Sixty-eight places of pilgrims – A reference to sixty-eight holy places for bathing for Hindu pilgrims in India

Sura – God

Vedas – Ancient Hindu scriptures

Yogi – One who practices Yoga

photo attribution

Figure 1: Guru Nanak with Japuji Sahib inscribed all over, 1880/1900.
Photo source:
https://artsandculture.google.com/asset/guru-nanak-ji-with-japuji-sahib-inscribed-all-over-unknown-sikh-school/bQERrsc07ANvjw
Attribution: Author unknown. Public domain.

Figure 2: Fresco of Guru Nanak from Baoli Sahib, Goindwal, circa 19th century.
Photo source:
https://sikhhistory.quora.com/The-lives-of-the-first-5-Gurus-according-to-me-Life-of-Guru-Nanak-Shah-Ji-The-life-of-Guru-Nanak-is-according-to-the-m?comment_id=10003768&comment_type=3
Attribution: Author unknown. Public domain.

Figure 3: Coin from 1747 CE depicting Guru Nanak with his two disciples, Bhai Mardana and Bhai Bala waving a chaur (fly-whisk) as a mark of respect.
Photo source:
https://commons.wikimedia.org/w/index.php?curid=87784178
Attribution: By Taha b. Wasiq b. Hussain, Own work, CC BY-SA 4.0.

Figure 4: From a 17th-century copy of the Guru Granth Sahib.
Photo source:
https://lakhvir.wordpress.com/2006/07/11/
rarely-seen-images-of-the-sikh-past-part-i/
Attribution: Photographer unknown. Public domain.

Figure 5:
Original handwritten Stanza 1 by Mrs. Pushpa Bakshi.
Attribution: Bakshi Archives Image.

Figure 6: Original typewritten page of translation typed by Mr. Om Prakash Bakshi.
Attribution: Bakshi Archives Image.

Figure 7: Folio of the Japuji Sahib from the Kartarpur Bir, penned by Bhai Gurdas.
Photo source:
https://commons.wikimedia.org/wiki/File:Folio_of_the_Japji_Sahib_composition_of_the_Kartarpur_Bir.jpg
Attribution: Guru Arjan and Bhai Gurdas. Public domain.

Figure 8: Mural of Guru Nanak presenting and chanting the Japuji Sahib in the presence of Guru Angad with Bhai Bala to side with a fly-whisk, circa 19th century.
Photo Source:
https://commons.wikimedia.org/wiki/File:Mural_of_Guru_Nanak_presenting_the_Japji_Sahib_to_Guru_Angad_with_Bhai_Bala_to_side_with_a_fly-whisk,_circa_19th_century.jpg
Attribution: This is a faithful photographic reproduction of a two-dimensional, public domain work of art. Unknown artist.

Figure 9: Opening verses of the Japuji Sahib composition of Guru Nanak inscribed on a plate of the 'Charaina' body armour containing verses from the Guru Granth Sahib and Dasam Granth inscribed on each plate. The armor was worn by Guru Gobind Singh in the battle of Bhangani, ca.1688. Collection of the royal family of the former state of Patiala.
Photo Source:
https://twitter.com/SikhScope/status/1523123099452907520
Attribution: This is a faithful photographic reproduction of a two-dimensional, public domain work of art. Photographer unknown. Author unknown.

Figure 10: Illuminated Adi Granth folio with nisan of Guru Gobind Singh. Lahore recension, late 17th to early 18th century. Collection of Takht Sri Harimandir Sahib, Patna.
Photo Source:
http://www.sikhiwiki.org/index.php
Attribution: This is a faithful photographic reproduction of a two-dimensional, public domain work of art. Photographed by Jeevan Singh Deol. Author unknown.

Figure 11: Guru Granth Sahib manuscript housed at Sri Keshgarh Sahib, Anandpur. Dated to 1803 B.S. (1746 C.E.).
Photo Source:
'Shabad Guru: Illustrated Catalogue of Rare Guru Granth Sahib Manuscripts' Volume I (2011) by Mohinder Singh, via URL: https://twitter.com/moomjamma/status/1166054955356237827
Attribution: This is a faithful photographic reproduction of a two-dimensional, public domain work of art. Unknown scribe. Photographed by Mohinder Singh.

Figure 12: A rare early 19th century mural painting from Gurdwara Baba Atal depicting Guru Nanak. Mid to late 19th century.

Photo Source: https://commons.wikimedia.org/wiki/File:Mural_painting_ of_Guru_Nanak_from_Gurdwara_Baba_Atal_Rai.jpg

Attribution: This is a faithful photographic reproduction of a two-dimensional, public domain work of art. Photographed by Amritpal Singh Mann. Painted by Jaimal Singh Naqqash (1860–1916), Mehtab Singh Naqqash (1871–1940), and Hukum Singh. This file is licensed under the Creative Commons Attribution-Share Alike 4.0 International license.

Figure 13: Identified handwriting of Guru Nanak from the Guru Harsahai Pothi. Early 16th century.

Photo Source: http://www.giss.org/sikh_panth.html

Attribution: This is a faithful photographic reproduction of a two-dimensional, public domain work of art. Unknown photographer. Author: Guru Nanak.

Figure 14: The Gurdwara Janam Asthan in Nankana Sahib, Pakistan—the site where Nanak is believed to have been born.

Photo Source: https://commons.wikimedia.org/wiki/File:The_Entrance_of_ Janam_Asthan-2.jpg

Attribution: Photographer: Shaguftakarim, CC BY-SA 4.0, https://commons.wikimedia.org/w/index. php?curid=51754062.

Figure 15: A Minaret of Gurdwara Janam Asthan.
Photo Source:
https://commons.wikimedia.org/wiki/File:The_Minaret_of_ Gurdwara_Janam_Asthan.jpg
Attribution: Photographer: Shaguftakarim, CC BY-SA 4.0, https://commons.wikimedia.org/w/index. php?curid=51754062.

Figure 16: Birth of Guru Nanak, painting from an 1830's Janamsakhi.
Photo Source:
https://commons.wikimedia.org/wiki/File:Birth_of_Guru_ Nanak,_painting_from_an_1830%27s_Janamsakhi_(life_sto-ries)_13.jpg
Attribution: By Unknown author. 1830's Janamsakhi, Public Domain.

Figure 17: Bhai Mani Singh's Janamsakhi (biographical sourc-es on Guru Nanak's life) was originally written in 1712. This reproduction is likely circa 19th century.
Photo Source:
https://commons.wikimedia.org/wiki/File:Bhai_Mani_Sing-h%27s_Janamsakhi.jpg
Attribution: Unknown author. Panjab Digital Library, Public domain.

Figure 18: Mr. Om Prakash Bakshi in his study at his resi-dence, 1/121 Capper Road, Lalbagh, Lucknow, Uttar Pradesh, India, circa 1958.
Attribution: Bakshi Archives Image.

Figure 19: Mrs. Pushpa Bakshi (wife of the author and mother of the editor), circa 1956.
Attribution: Bakshi Archives Image.

Figure 20: Mr. Om Prakash Bakshi and Mrs. Pushpa Bakshi, team behind the translation, circa 1956.
Attribution: Bakshi Archives Image.

Figure 21: Editor Vivek Bakshi with his parents at the terrace of their residence, 1/121 Capper Road, Lalbagh, Lucknow, Uttar Pradesh, India, circa 1975.
Attribution: Bakshi Archives Image.

Figure 22: Mr. Om Prakash Bakshi with his three elder brothers, circa late 1970s - early 1980s.
Attribution: Bakshi Archives Image.

Figure 23: Mrs. Kartar Devi Kaur, a devout Sikh and grandmother of the editor, circa 1970s.
Attribution: Bakshi Archives Image.

www.ingramcontent.com/pod-product-compliance
Lightning Source LLC
Chambersburg PA
CBHW040845120626

46547CB00001B/34